ECONOMIC THEORY

ECONOMIC THEORY
A Critic's Companion

SECOND REVISED EDITION

M.A.G. van Meerhaeghe
(University of Ghent)

1986 SPRINGER-SCIENCE+BUSINESS MEDIA, B.V.

Library of Congress Cataloging in Publication Data

Meerhaeghe, Marcel Alfons Gilbert van, 1921-
Economic theory.

Includes bibliographies and indexes.
1. Economics. I. Title.
HB171.5.M5112 1986 330 86-16295
ISBN 978-94-017-1367-2 ISBN 978-94-017-1365-8 (eBook)
DOI 10.1007/978-94-017-1365-8

Book Information

First published 1980 by Martinus Nijhoff, Boston.

Souvent l'appareil savant ne cache que le besoin d'étonner et de se faire valoir: au bout du compte, ce qu'on trouve, l'homme de bon sens le savait déjà.

J.-P. HAESAERT

CONTENTS

PREFACE

The content of this book formed part of an introduction to economics. Weidenfeld and Nicolson published an english translation in 1971: *Economics. A critical approach.* Since several colleagues thought that the critical comments on various theories might discourage students, I divided this introduction into two parts. Wereas the first part deals with economic theory as such, the present publication contains the subject matter of the second part, namely the former appraisal sections. The first edition benefited from comment by Professor P. Hennipman, who, although I took his comment into consideration as far as possible, did not always share my views.

The appendix to the first edition (Economic Doctrines) has been omitted. I have used brief portions of it in a new chapter, 'Economic doctrines and economic policy'. I have added a chapter entitled 'Economic theory and economic policy' and brought up to date the other chapters.

This book has no intention of instructing fellow economists. It is intended as a complement to an introductory course on economics, which for the most part does not deal systematically with (or is even totally lacking in) critical comments.

Many economists consider any criticism of economic theory to be a form of *lèse-majesté.* On the other hand, a critical approach should not be the monopoly of left-wing authors.

I have been assisted by members of my staff in tracking down new literature of interest for this book and in reading proofs. Miss Greet Caluwaerts compiled the indexes and completed some bibliographical references. As in the first edition Mr. John Cairns, FIL, handled the linguistic aspects. My wife has given me considerable help. She also read the proofs. I am very grateful to all of them.

M.A.G. v. M.

1. INTRODUCTION

Economic science has always been the subject of criticism, especially during the depression of the thirties and after the Second World War, when I, among others, deplored that: '. . . so much energy was wasted in obtaining so few results, or in discussing matters of practically no importance.'[1]

In 1955 an excellent summary of the 'failures' of economics by S. Schoeffler was published;[2] subsequently Guy Routh traced the 'origins of economic ideas' and explained the survival of outdated disparate ideas.[3]

In 1958, P. Hennipman stated: 'For some time now, more and more symptoms of serious discontent and concern about the present state and recent development of economic science have been observed.'[4] This sentence, with which he opened a thorough and erudite essay on 'Recent criticism of economic science', applies with even greater force in the present situation.

Books and numerous articles have since been devoted to the 'crisis', e.g., the not so original works of A. Lowe,[5] B. Ward[6] and the less coherent publication of J. Robinson.[7] In the eighties, the first edition of this book,[8] Balogh's 'Irrelevance of conventional economics'[9] and collections of articles (which precludes a systematic exposition): *The crisis in economic theory,*[10] *The crisis in economic theories*[11] and *Economics in disarray.*[12]

Before embarking in the following chapters upon a critique of economic science, I shall enlarge upon terminological confusion and plagiarism, ailments that afflict economics as well as other social sciences. Finally, attention shall be drawn to the relationship between ideology and economics and to rationality. I will not follow the conventional distinction between micro- and macro-economic theory, since they are too interrelated to be treated separately.

I. TERMINOLOGY

The lack of unanimity concerning the definition of economics is quite normal. Other social sciences are also in search of a definition. Some authors simply put forward the view that 'Economics is what economists do',[13] or 'Economics is the study of economics'.[14] The controversy between the champions of the various definitions, according to W. Eucken a 'useless battle', has in any case yielded few results.[15]

But the absense of agreement on the meaning of the concepts used in a science is more serious. And unfortunately, in economics the simplest concepts are defined in numerous and divergent ways. For example, one need only point to the number of different meanings of *capital* and *capitalism*; the same applies to economic structure (some authors consider technological knowledge as a structural element, others do not), national product, national wealth; and finally, endless terminological disputes have arisen from the link between *saving* and *investment.* At a conference 'it became evident that even the assembled experts were using some terms familiar to all of them in different senses'.[16]

My complaint is by no means original. In the last century, Malthus spoke of the defective formulation of concepts in economics, [17] and in 1937 R. Miry wrote:

> ... It would be hard to dream up a bigger muddle than the terminology we employ. In many cases we do not even understand each other because we assign the most varied meanings to one and the same word. We are living in a tower of Babel ... continuously aggravated by acrobatic terms which we forge in order to look more learned than a colleague or to have the air of saying something different from a predecessor.[18]

Ten years later, J.S. Davis was warning us:

> If economics is to deserve recognition as a science, even in the modest sense of orderly arrangement of better knowledge, we need to do better in choosing and clarifying elementary concepts, standardizing terms, and becoming more explicit and consistent in our use of both.[19]

and C.F. Carter joins him when he speaks of economics as an 'immensely complex subject, with no agreed notation or set of definitions.'[20]

And when there is a certain agreement on a concept, economists often lose sight of the fact that interpretation of the concept is difficult. This can be illustrated by the following examples.

International comparisons of statistics on the national product must be made with caution, not only due to the divergent relative importance of incomes of, for example, members of the armed forces and intermediaries in the distribution process, but also because the accuracy with which the national product is calculated varies considerably from country to country (and exchange rates do not reflect economic reality).

In most of the less-developed countries a good deal of juggling is needed to draw up national income statistics. The less-developed countries are not as poor as the figures suggest. In those countries untraded goods are cheaper than in the developed countries. A comparison between the real income of India and that of the United Kingdom shows that the former figure is 234 percent higher than the amount that would be obtained by converting the money income of both countries into a common currency.[21]

Partial productivity (the ratio of output to a single factor, e.g. labour, both expressed in money terms) as a yardstick of economic efficiency is significant only if there has been no factor substitution (or change in the factor combination). Even then, it is doubtful whether the value of the different types of labour (which, moreover, do not remain unchanged) can be added up.

F. Schaller correctly observes that in the literature we can find the most varied formulas for measuring productivity, but that the real difficulty is to establish what productivity is, what the object of our research is, and what precise significance we ought to attribute to the information found.[22] One therefore wonders whether it would not be preferable to substitute the neutral expression 'production per unit of input of labour' for 'productivity' and 'labour productivity'.

2. ORIGINALITY

To avoid bringing out old theories, a better knowledge of earlier authors is required. Far too often in economics, conclusions that were already formulated a long time ago are drawn triumphantly. Ignorance – even among well-known authors – is not always the only explanation. Sometimes plagiarism is committed without the least compunction. In this connection, P.A. Sorokin speaks of 'amnesia' and the 'discoverer's complex'. He writes: 'The younger generation of sociologists and psychologists', (and he could just as well have added economists), 'explicitly claims that nothing important has been discovered in their field during all the preceding centuries; . . . and that the real scientific era . . . began only in the last two or three decades with the publication of their own researches . . .'.[23] Hence, the definition of the historian of economic thought as a 'Sadist who delights in pointing out to graduate students and colleagues that their brilliant ideas are not original'.[24]

I have therefore endeavoured – often by numerous quotations – to disclaim originality concerning what has already been said by others.

By this I do not mean that only original works are of value; the desire for originality leads not only to plagiarism, voluntary or involuntary, but also to many publications that should never have seen the light of day. In this respect, G.J. Stigler is right when he states:

> that we commonly exaggerate the merits of originality in economics – that we are unjust in conferring immortality upon the authors of absurd theories while we forget the fine, if not particularly original, work of others.[25]

Vauvenargues was correct in stating that 'It is easier to put forward new ideas than to conciliate those advanced earlier'.[26]

3. IDEOLOGY

Marxists in particular have repeatedly charged that economics is at the service of liberal concepts and that it nurtures extreme individualism and anti-interventionism. In particular, they have in mind hypotheses such as perfect competition, upon which many economic theories are based. This does not, of course, connote economists who because of '. . . their connection with definite parties and pressure groups . . . shut their eyes to the remoter consequences of the policies they are advocating',[27] but the practitioners of economic science who are not at the service of any interest group.

Marx himself upbraided economists for being the scientific representatives of the bourgeoisie.[28] G. Myrdal points out the value judgments that have existed in economic literature since the early physiocrats. These value judgments determine the choice of both the problems treated and the method applied. Myrdal would like every personal preference to be expressed as such, rather than as the result of a nonevaluative economic analysis.[29] In other words, a neutral science is out of the question; F.L. Polak also holds that opinion.[30] P. Dieterlen is no less decisive: 'The economist is an ideologist who accepts or fights himself as such, but then ignores himself. The *no* with which he answers the ideologists around him is neither more nor less ideological than their *yes*'.[31] Other contemporary economists such as K. Boulding[32] and R. Harrod[33] also acknowledge value judgments.[34]

According to the Soviet official textbook on economics, a neutral economic science does not exist; economics is a party science: '... only a political economy which upholds the interests of the working class can ... be objective and disinterested'.[35]

Most economists admit that observations are being influenced not only by the intrinsic characteristics of the observed phenomena, but also – unconsciously – by the mirror through which we see the world. Thus observations may also be influenced by social bias and education.[36] In other words, they accept the existence of an ideological bias, 'though, like Marx, they find it only in others and never in themselves; but they do not admit that it is an inescapable curse and that it vitiates economics to its core'.[37]

Confrontation with value judgments here, there and everywhere makes any objective knowledge impossible. If the choice of certain subjects of study or hypotheses[38] and the emphasis that is laid on analysis in the short or in the long run can be explained by ideological and psychological factors, this does not mean that their scientific significance is thereby impaired. They must 'in any case ... be judged independently of those subjective elements, and according to their own tendency'.[39] Ideological factors may indeed be stimulating. K.R. Popper even argues that 'The objective and neutral scientist ... is not the ideal scientist. Being a scientist without motivation is no good, not even in exact sciences'.[40] Divergent points of view are not necessarily due to value judgments:

> ... often a certain unavoidable allowance for divergent personal opinions exists ... because it is impossible to determine all relevant, and for the solution of the problem necessary, facts and relations. But then, the researchers' subjective latency is not the primary cause of such differences of opinion.[41]

According to the generally accepted view, economic science does not become involved in the definition of targets; it takes them for granted and only says how they must be achieved.[42] Prominent among those who plead for a nonevaluative economic analysis is Max Weber,[43] although he admits that it is an unattainable ideal. The critics mentioned above call this neutrality ethically objectionable: it is alleged to imply indifference to society.[44] However, this overlooks the difference between economic science and its application. Every economist has the right to have his or her own opinion on the targets of economic policy. Nevertheless, the economist is expected to state his or her value judgments clearly. A socialist and a liberal economist pursue differing aims; what one of them accepts as normal is unacceptable to the other. But liberal and socialist or Marxist economies are nonexistent.

In recent times, more and more voices have been calling for a more active approach by the economist. The latter is required to be involved in current problems. More specifically, the economist is expected to be interested in the reformation of present-day society. 'Today's fashion often hesitates between two opinions difficult to reconcile: arguing in favour of involvement but against scientists having their hands tied'.[45] Indeed, the two generally go together. F. Hartog rightly points out that there is no danger of a lack of 'involvement', but of a 'critical distance from which, free of all attachments, only the truth is aimed at'. He therefore argues in favour of a 'free, critical, fundamental and objective study of science in general and of economics in particular'.[46] From what has just been stated it follows that this attitude is not easy to adopt. More than any other science, economics must guard against the influence of political convictions on theory.

4. RATIONALITY

Rational economic action implies in the case of 'homo oeconomicus' that he seeks as a consumer maximum utility, as an entrepreneur maximum profit, and as a representative of government the maximization of general welfare. He has to apply the economic principle: with given means he attains as many objectives as possible, or he fulfils his (given) objectives with a minimum of means. Here a classification of needs is called for and the most urgent ones are satisfied first.

The person acting according to the economic principle does not necessarily act infallibly: he *thinks* that he acts rationally. If the consumer's actual choice is considered the rational choice, the notion of rational action loses its significance. The economic principle becomes '... entirely neutral and empty, such an innocent hypothesis ... that it is useless as a psychological premise'.[47] If this concept is adopted man always acts rationally. In that case rational action is rather modal action.

H.Simon coined the term 'bounded rationality' to indicate that economic actors are not hyperrational. As a consequence of 'bounded rationality' and of opportunism they differ from economic man 'in that they are less competent in calculation and less trustworthy and reliable in action'.[48] The consumer, for example, does not know the amount or the prices of the available commodities.

NOTES

1 M. van Meerhaeghe, De la théorie à la politique économique.La comptabilité nationale, *Industrie. Revue de la Fédération des Industries belges,* April 1950, p. 203.

2 S. Schoeffler, *The failures of economics* (Cambridge, Mass.: Harvard University Press, 1955).

3 G. Routh, *The origin of economic ideas* (London: Macmillan, 1975).

4 P. Hennipman, Critiques récentes de la science économique, *Bulletin d'Information et de Documentation de la Banque Nationale de Belgique,* April 1958, p. 249.

5 A. Lowe, *On economic knowledge. Towards a science of political economics* (New York: Harper and Row, 1965).

6 B. Ward, *What's wrong with economics?* (New York: Macmillan, 1972).

7 J. Robinson, *Economic heresies. Some old-fashioned questions in economic theory* (New York: Basic Books, 1971); id., The second crisis of economic theory, *The American Economic Review,* May 1972.

8 M.A.G. van Meerhaeghe, *Economic theory. A critic's companion* (Boston: Martinus Nijhoff, 1980); see also M.A.G. van Meerhaeghe, *Economics. A critical approach* (London: Weidenfeld & Nicolson, 1971).

9 T. Balogh, *Irrelevance of conventional economics* (London: Weidenfeld & Nicolson, 1982).

10 *The crisis in economic theory,* ed. D. Bell and I. Kristol (New York: Basic Books, 1981).

11 *The crisis in economic theories,* ed. G. Caravale (Milan: F. Angeli, 1983).

12 *Economics in disarray,* ed. P. Wiles and G. Routh (London: Macmillan, 1984).

13 K.E. Boulding, *Economics as a science* (New York: McGraw-Hill, 1970), p. 97.

14 D. Seers, The limitations of the special case, in *Leading issues in economic development, Studies in international poverty,* ed. G.M. Meier 2nd ed. (New York: Oxford University Press, 1970), p. 68.

15 W. Eucken, *Die Grundlagen der Nationalökonomie,* 7th ed. (Berlin: J. Springer, 1959), p. 29.

16 W.S. Salant, A partial glossary of international finance, in *European monetary unification and its meaning for the United States,* ed. L.B. Krause and W.S. Salant (Washington: The Brookings Institution, 1973), p. 310.

17 T. Malthus, *Definitions in political economy* (London: Murray, 1827), preface.

18 R. Miry, Vraagtekens en tekortkomingen, *Tijdschrift voor Economie en Sociologie,* Oct. 1937, p. 359.

19 J.S. Davis, Whither now? in *Economic research and the development of economic*

science and public policy (New York: National Bureau of Economic Research, 1946), p. 179.

20 C.F. Carter, preface in R.E. Emmer, *Economic analysis and scientific philosophy* (London: George Allen and Unwin, 1967), p. 9.

21 I.B. Kravis, A.W. Heston and R. Summers, Real GDP per capita for more than one hundred countries, *The Economic Journal,* June 1978, p. 216. See also D. Usher,*Rich and poor countries. A study in problems of comparisons of real income* (London: Institute of Economic Affairs, 1966).

22 F. Schaller, Qu'est-ce que la productivité?, *Rivista Internazionale di Scienze Economiche e Commerciali,* May 1969.

23 P.A. Sorokin, *Fads and foibles in modern sociology and related sciences* (Chicago: Henry Regnery 1956), p. 3.

24 R. Brandis, An irreverent glossary, *Journal of Economic Issues,* Sept. 1972, p. 108.

25 G.S. Stigler, The nature and role of originality in scientific progress, *Economica,* Nov. 1955, p. 302.

26 L. de Vauvenargues, *Réflexions et maximes, 2nd ed.* (Paris: Croville, 1934), p. 29.

27 L. von Mises, *Human action. A treatise of economics* (Chicago: William Hodge, 1949), p. 865.

28 K. Marx, *The poverty of philosophy* 1847 – Eng. ed. (New York: International Publishers, 1963), Chap. 2.

29 G. Myrdal, *The political element in the development of economic theory* (London: Routledge and Kegan Paul, 1955); this book was first published in Swedish (1930) and in German (1933). See its Book Review by F. Machlup in *The American Economic Review,* Dec. 1955. See also G. Myrdal, *Value in social theory. A selection of essays on methodology* (London: Routledge and Kegan Paul, 1958).

30 F.L. Polak, *Kennen en keuren in de sociale wetenschappen. Een onderzoek naar de afbakening van objectieve en subjectieve oordelen in de economie, tevens een proeve van critiek op de wetenschapsleer van Max Weber* (Leiden: H.E. Stenfert Kroeze, 1948).

31 P. Dieterlen, *L'idéologie économique* (Paris: Cujas, 1964), p. 280.

32 K. Boulding, op. cit., p. 119.

33 R. Harrod, Scope and method of economics, *The Economic Journal,* Sept. 1938.

34 See also B. Ward, op. cit., p. 198.

35 *Manuel d'économie politique* (Paris: Ed. Sociales, 1965),, p. 16 [Eng. ed.: Political economy: A textbook (London: Laurence and Wishart, 1957].

36 During more than 40 years Benjamin Constant collected 10,000 facts, which were to be embodied in an antireligious work. After having changed his mind on religion, those facts still remained useful: 'They were inversed . . . and plead now in the opposite sense'. Example from C. Colson, *Cours d'économie politique* (Paris: Gauthier-Villars 1924), p. 135, cited by A. Marchal, *Méthode scientifique et science économique* (Paris: M.-Th. Génin, 1955), p. 62.

37 J.A. Schumpeter, Science and ideology, *The American Economic Review,* March 1949, p. 349.

38 Thus, a liberal economist usually does not accept that private investments are inadequate, because this assumption could lead to more state intervention.

39 P. Hennipman, art. cit., p. 252.

40 K.R. Popper, Die Logik der Sozialwissenschaften, *Kölner Zeitschrift für Soziologie und Sozialpsychologie,* Sept. 1962, p. 242.

41 P. Hennipman, art. cit., p. 253.

42 This modern conception is in contrast to the classical conception (the task of economic policy is to raise national output as high as possible) and to the more extensive, normative conception (noneconomic standards must also be complied with). See P. Hennipman, Doel-

einden en criteria der economische politiek, in *Theorie van de economische politiek,* ed. J.E. Andriessen and M.A.G. van Meerhaeghe (Leiden: Stenfert Kroese, 1962), p. 66.

43 M. Weber, *The methodology of the social sciences* (Glencoe, Ill.: The Free Press, 1949). Previously the physiocrats and classic authors assumed a normative point of view.

44 See, for instance, F.L. Polak, op. cit., p. 267.

45 F. Hartog, Onthechting, *Economisch-Statistische Berichten,* Dec. 6, 1972, p. 1159.

46 Ibid., p. 1159.

47 P. Hennipman, *Economisch motief en economisch principe* (Amsterdam: Noord-Nederlandsche Uitgeversmaatschappij, 1945), p. 362.

48 H.A. Simon, *Models of man. Social and rational mathematical essays on rational human behavior in a social setting* (New York: John Wiley, 1957), p. 198.

2. THE THEORY OF CONSUMER'S BEHAVIOUR

Since the theory of the consumer's behaviour is founded mainly on Gossen's 'laws' or on the indifference curves, these are discussed first, followed by demand and the consumption and saving functions.

I. GOSSEN'S 'LAWS'

Exceptions to the first 'law' (marginal utility declines as more units are added) seem not infrequent; for instance, if one drinks a second glass of beer immediately after the first then the second may provide greater utility than the first. But the consumer does not know the amount of the marginal utility – not measurable – yielded by the consumption of the last unit of a good (quite apart from whether or not the concept is familiar).

The second law states that the marginal utilities of the goods purchased must be proportional to the outlays needed to acquire them. But the consumer has only imperfect knowledge of the prices of different goods. And in any case, no scholarly comparison of marginal utilities is made. It would, in fact, be difficult to attain equality in the ratios because of the limited divisibility or the indivisibility of most goods. Yet the consumer is said unconsciously to aim at equal ratios.

Much of the consumer's behaviour is the result of traditions and habits determined by social environment; however, this does not necessarily have adverse consequences as it enables the consumer to reduce his transaction costs (e.g. for clothes).[1] The consumer normally adheres to a set pattern of consumption (although he may like a change *per se* in his consumption pattern), but changes in prices or in income do exercise a certain influence. Some purchases may be motivated by impulse or emotion (e.g. when the consumer buys goods impulsively). In that case, as J. Marchal has put it, the consumer is much more 'l'homme de Pavlov' than 'l'homme de Descartes.[2] The consumer only takes time to buy a limited number of goods (usually expensive goods for which he or she is willing to incur high transaction costs), and is also influenced by incidentals. On the other hand, money may be spent liberally on commodities such as makeup.

Moreover, when a consumer purchases various goods, the situation or the opinion of the other consumers is constantly taken into consideration. Greater satisfaction of wants is no synonym for greater (total) utility or more happiness;[3] if satisfaction of the wants of others has increased to a greater extent, the consumer does not have the feeling that total utility has been enhanced. In order to secure greater prestige, one can, on the one hand, aim at wealth and/or political power, or, on the other hand, promote charitable activities.

Utility is a relative, not an absolute, concept. The fact is that interpersonal utility comparison is not possible, precisely because utility is not measurable. Gossen's 'laws' are therefore to a great extent unrealistic.

E. Wagemann was not exaggerating when he complained about 'how much ingenuity and trouble has been expended in speculating about marginal utilities'.[4]

2. THE INDIFFERENCE CURVES

To circumvent the difficulty that utility cannot be measured, *indifference curves* are often used. That a consumers' scale of preference is given (and cannot be influenced) – as is assumed in the theory of indifference curves – is not in accordance with reality. Hence, K. Boulding considers the doctrine of 'the Immaculate Conception of the indifference curve' as 'one of the most peculiar illusions of economists'.[5]

It is also doubtful whether the consumer can distinguish between the numerous indifferent situations. Indeed, how can the consumer know that two combinations are indifferent, if their utility is not known? The consumer buys the different goods in more or less constant ratios. In any case, there is no point in assuming unlimited substitutability among the goods. The fact that this tool of analysis is not very realistic becomes even clearer when it is extended and used for more than two goods: How could the consumer possibly distinguish between the thousands of possible combinations? In 1932 H. Mayer pointed out:

> The more goods contained in a combination and the more heterogeneous those goods, the more grotesque the consequences that flow from the fiction that as we consume less bread or meat we will consume more salt, that every reduction in the amount of tea consumed is offset by an increase

> in the amount of sugar consumed in the equivalent (indifferent) daily combinations, the less furniture the more rooms, the less heating material the more aesthetic pleasure, the less clothing the more cigarettes, and so on. More clearly than any abstract argument, these absurd deductions expose the wholly unempirical nature of the supposedly empirical assumptions on which the construction of indifference curves is based.[6]

As with marginal utility, we have to bear in mind the fact that the available money is not necessarily *entirely* spent, and that most goods are indivisible and not homogeneous – still other assumptions on which the doctrine of the indifference curves is based. Indivisibility finds particularly marked expression in the expensive consumption goods of which only one unit is normally purchased (car, refrigerator). Even if a second unit is purchased, the consumer goes for diversity and generally chooses a different model: The neighbours must notice the second acquisition. In fact, not only different commodities are compared but also different qualities of the same commodity (each quality constituting a different product).

Indifference curves are useful only in the analysis of problems of choice of a limited kind (e.g. between present and future consumption, between material possessions and leisure). However, they are not observable phenomena.

To obviate this drawback, P.A. Samuelson has suggested[7] basing analysis on consumer preferences as expressed in market conduct, or actual purchases – the theory of revealed preferences (as opposed to the *latent* preferences). Even here it is very difficult to draw the relevant curves or behaviour lines, since they would have to take account of large variations in income in order to reveal the associated preferences. If compatible with income, durable goods may be bought all at once or in a given sequence; then nothing is revealed. Moreover, one observation is not sufficient. (The same preference may not result.) Here again, one often forgets that wants are changeable and that the consumer's purchases are determined by habit, not by minor fluctuations in income. So far, this approach has not been fruitful in empirical research.[8]

We therefore agree with E.J. Mishan when he describes these theories of the consumer's behaviour as 'an unnecessary adornment on the apparatus of economic analysis'[9] and with L.C. Thurow when he writes that revealed preference 'is just a fancy way of saying that individuals do whatever individuals do'.[10]

3. THE INFLUENCE OF THE OTHER CONSUMERS

As I have pointed out above, there is an interrelationship of the satisfaction of wants of various households. The quantity demanded for a given product sometimes increases because people notice that it is being bought by other consumers, and people are always ready to imitate their fellows. In other cases, the quantity demanded falls when we see other consumers buying a product. (We do not want to imitate and wish to purchase another product.) H. Leibenstein calls these phenomena the 'bandwagon effect' and the 'snob effect'.[11] A 'snob effect' can turn into a 'bandwagon effect'.

They should not be confused with the 'demonstration effect':[12] When we come into contact with better quality products previously unknown to us, we buy them and our consumption expenditure goes up even if our income has remained unchanged. In point of fact, the bandwagon effect and the demonstration effect usually coincide, because the latter occurs while one is observing other people's consumption.

Finally, reference may be made under this head to the Veblen effect:[13] demand increases because price goes up, since the consumer wishes to demonstrate the ability to buy expensive goods (conspicuous consumption).

4. DEMAND

By demand, in economics, we mean the series of quantities of a good that we are prepared to buy in the future at a given time or within a specified short period at various (hypothetical) prices.

The construction of demand schedules and demand curves is, however, very difficult. F. Machlup has called the operation a 'tour de force'.[14] Indeed, it requires us to establish the reactions of a consumer (or a group of consumers) to the different prices all ruling at the same moment. As this is impossible, we are obliged to rely on assumptions or to study the amounts actually demanded at *different times.* The latter method is dangerous because the other circumstances that are assumed to remain the same change, in fact, even when the period of observation is relatively short. On the whole, the innumerable attempts to establish demand curves empirically have not met with success.[15]

Even when we are able to obtain satisfactory results, there is nothing to say that our demand curve will not be completely different the following day. It seems hardly likely that the consumer considers what his or her reactions would be if other, hypothetical, prices existed for the innumerable goods available on the market. If this is the case, the consumer will still think in terms of the actual price and investigate only a small number of possibilities with his price forecasts within a limited range (price fluctuations of, say, 10 percent). It is sometimes assumed that the consumer has two limit prices in mind for a restricted number of commodities – a minimum price below which a reliable product could not be supplied, and a maximum price above which the product is too expensive. The demand curve would then consist of a few points only.

Price changes do influence purchases of consumer durables by new consumers, but not so much the purchases of consumers who already possess the product in question. The further the price goes down the more readily will the latter replace durable goods (reducing the period of depreciation); at the same time they will be more likely to move over to a better quality product. The stocks and durability of consumer durables have an important effect on the choice of other goods.

In the demand schedule it is assumed that each price has to be considered as a datum. In other words, the buyer cannot influence the price by his or her purchase (because it represents a very small part of total purchases); this also implies that consumers' decisions are taken independently of each other (pure competition). Some buyers, however, are in a position to exert pressure on sellers; for instance, a cloister community, department stores and other big firms (although here we are examining households' demand, the concept also applies to the firms' demand for intermediate products). Finally, price is only one of the factors that influence demand. Hence, the distinction that is sometimes made, depending on the frequency and nature of purchases, between convenience goods, shopping goods and specialty goods.

Why economists accepted such a far from operational definition of demand (and related concepts such as price elasticity) is an enigma. Consequently, it is not surprising that some authors such as R.E. Emmer[16] argue that demand, if defined as above, does not exist.

5. CONSUMPTION AND SAVING

It is often asserted, following J.M. Keynes[17], that the marginal propensity to consume will gradually decline as income increases (this is known as the *absolute income hypothesis*). Consumption does go up as income rises, but not to the same extent. The consumption function, then, is represented by a rising curve gradually flattening out. However, J.S. Duesenberry[18] considers that because of the demonstration effect individual preferences cannot be regarded as given: They are affected by the behaviour of other consumers ('keeping up with the Joneses'). In this case, consumption increases in proportion to income; in other words, the consumption curve is a straight line. This 'relative income hypothesis' is also maintained by F. Modigliani.[19]

M. Friedman[20], for his part, maintains that saving always represents the same proportion of 'permanent' income and consumption (the *permanent income hypothesis*'), 'permanent' income including normal prospective income in succeeding periods. Fortuitous and temporary factors can result in lower actual earnings than the expected income (which is very hard to estimate statistically). F. Modigliani stresses 'permanent wealth' rather than 'permanent income' (life cycle theory). M. Feldstein has enlarged upon Modigliani's theory.[21] He argues that households will regard the discounted present value of future pensions as part of their wealth and adjust their direct saving accordingly.

What we have said about the demand curve also applies, mutadis mutandis, to the consumption and saving curves: It is difficult to construct these curves. Further, it is simplistic to explain consumption and saving curves mainly by income; they are too much affected by other circumstances that in theory are assumed to remain the same but never do (e.g. the income distribution and relative prices). This explains why empirical inquiries concerning the theories referred to previously have yielded disappointing and contradictory results. The consumption and saving functions are changing constantly, and what is true today may not hold tomorrow.

All this bears out the (still applicable) statement by A.F. Burns some forty years ago: '. . . our ability to forecast what increment of consumer outlay will accompany a specified increment of income . . . is as yet very limited'.[22]

6. CONCLUSION

The foregoing shows that little is certain about consumer behaviour. One is naturally not surprised that the constant efforts exerted in this field have yielded relatively meagre results.[23] M. Shubik deplores the existing theory being presented '... as though it were the relevant way to study consumer behavior, rather than one partially explored path in almost virgin territory.'[24]

NOTES

1 Transaction costs: costs involved in economic transactions, more particularly those concerning the obtaining of the required information, and the journey to and from the market place.

2 J. Marchal, Essai de révision de la théorie des prix à la lumière des progrès de la psychologie moderne, *Zeitschrift für Nationalökonomie,* Heft 2, 1949, p. 269.

3 Cf. T. Scitovski, *The joyless economy. An inquiry into human satisfaction and consumer dissatisfaction* (Oxford: Oxford University Press, 1976).

4 E. Wagemann, *Berühmte Denkfehler der Nationalökonomie* (Bern: A. Francke, 1951), p. 30.

5 K. Boulding, op. cit., p. 119.

6 H. Mayer, Der Erkenntniswert der funktionellen Preistheorie, in *Die Wirtschaftstheorie der Gegenwart,* vol. 2 (Wien: J. Springer, 1932), p. 73.

7 P. Samuelson, *Foundation of economic analysis* (Cambridge, Mass.: Harvard University Press, 1947); id., Consumption theorems in terms of overcompensation rather than indifference comparisons, *Economica,* Febr. 1953.

8 A.P. Barten, Trends in the analysis of consumer demand, in *25 years of economic theory. Retrospect and prospect* (Leiden: Martinus Nijhoff, 1976), p. 14.

9 E.J. Mishan, Theories of consumer behaviour: a cynical view, *Economica,* Febr. 1961, p. 5.

10 L.C. Thurow, *Dangerous currents. The state of economics* (New York: Random House, 1983), p. 267.

11 H. Leibenstein, Bandwagon, snob and Veblen effects in the theory of consumer's demand, *The Quarterly Journal of Economics,* May 1950.

12 J.S. Duesenberry, *Income, saving and the theory of consumer behavior* (Cambridge, Mass.: Harvard University Press, 1949).

13 T. Veblen, *The theory of the leisure class* (New York: Funk and Wagnalls, 1934), Chap. 4.

14 F. Machlup, Operationalism and pure theory in economics, in *The structure of economic science. Essays on methodology,* ed. S.R. Krupp (Englewood Cliffs, N.J.: Prentice-Hall, 1966), p. 63.

15 Cf. M. Friedman, *Price theory. A provisional text* (London: Frank Cass, 1982), pp. 33–34.

16 R.E. Emmer, op. cit., p. 98.

17 J.M. Keynes, *The general theory of employment, interest and money,* (London: MacMillan, 1936), Chap. 8.

18 J.S. Duesenberry, op. cit., p. 27.

19 F. Modigliani, Fluctuations in the saving-income ratio: a problem of economic forecasting, in *Studies in income and wealth,* pt. 11 (New York: National Bureau of Economic Research, 1949), p. 385.

20 M. Friedman, *A theory of the consumption function* (Princeton: Princeton University Press, 1957), p. 20.

21 M. Feldstein, Social security, induced retirement and aggregate capital accumulation, *The Journal of Political Economy*, 1974.

22 A.F. Burns, *Economic research and the Keynesian thinking of our times* (New York: National Bureau of Economic Research, 1946), p. 18.

23 D. Wood in a Note on new books in *The Economic Journal*, Sept. 1972, p. 1073.

24 M. Shubik, A curmudgeon's guide to micro-economics, *The Journal of Economic Literature*, June 1970, p. 410.

3. THE THEORY OF PRODUCER'S BEHAVIOUR

Because many theories are based on the assumption of complete substitutability, this concept will be studied first. After evaluating the optimum combination of factors of production and the optimum level of production, we will discuss supply and the investment decision.

I. SUBSTITUTABILITY AND COMPLEMENTARITY OF PRODUCTION FACTORS

Complete substitutability is nonexistent because factors are not entirely divisible. Machines have fixed capacities. Let us take a plant in which two different machines are needed to produce a certain good. If one has a capacity of 2 cwt, and the other a capacity of 4 cwt, part of the second machine's capacity will be idle if the plant produces 3 cwt. The same holds true of the labour input. In fact, only a limited number of combinations are possible. In the long run as well, complete substitutability does not exist.

Because the assumption of complete substitutability is highly suitable for mathematical analysis (e.g. the Cobb-Douglas production function), most studies proceed on it.

In fact, we find neither complete substitutability nor a constant ratio between the factors of production. The law of variable returns makes this evident. Increasing returns are in a sense explained by the indivisibility of the constant factor: the proportion of one factor to another may not immediately be what is wanted; after the best combination has been achieved, the relationship will again become unsatisfactory. The 'law' simply expresses the fact 'that there is a limit to the extent to which one factor of production can be substituted for another'.[1] The validity of the 'law' depends upon the successively added units being homogeneous, and this is not always the case.

2. THE OPTIMUM COMBINATION OF FACTORS FOR A GIVEN LEVEL OF OUTPUT

Where factors are substitutable, the cheapest of the possible combinations for producing a given quantity must be selected. The cheapest combination is that at which the marginal productivity of each additional unit of money spent on the factors is the same. If different additional sums (always assumed to be very small) are spent, then the respective marginal productivities should be proportional to them. When we are considering two factors alone, then the optimum combination can be found by means of *isoquants* (a curve which represents different combinations of the factors of production yielding the same quantity of output).

Since marginal productivities are difficult to calculate and isoquants even more difficult to work out, this method does not provide much of a basis on which to determine the optimum combination of factors. Moreover, the incomplete divisibility of factors limits its validity.

Longer term considerations can also play a part. When, for example, the speed with which a specified volume of production can be reached is considered important, entrepreneurs in less-developed countries are sometimes obliged to have recourse to capital-intensive methods. This may also be warranted if the firm can count on a wide market.

The theory also assumes that a change in the price of one factor has no influence on the price of another factor. However, this is not the case.

In point of fact, firms generally go by trial and error – starting out from an existing set of circumstances and seeing what happens when they make a (small) change in the combination of factors – or else they rely on experience built up by other firms. In certain cases, it is also possible to make use of linear programming (whenever there is a linear relationship between input and production, as is sometimes the case).

3. OPTIMUM LEVEL OF PRODUCTION

According to current economic theory we must determine the additional revenue and additional cost of producing an additional infinitesimal quantity. As long as marginal revenue is greater than marginal cost, increasing output will increase profits (at least in the rising part of the marginal cost curve). We therefore continue to produce up to the point where marginal cost equals marginal revenue.

Marginal cost and marginal revenue are, however, difficult to calculate, and – furthermore – many entrepreneurs are not conversant with the concepts. So the entrepreneur would have to compare the total revenue and the total cost corresponding to each level of production. Where the difference is greatest, he or she no longer has any interest in expanding production. In practice, however, the optimum level of output *sold* is generally established from the gross profits per unit (the difference between the selling price and the variable costs per unit).

The production level is then regarded as a function of sales. Methods of computing the optimum sales level include break-even point analysis and direct costing[2] – the two not being mutually exclusive.

Break-even analysis does not indicate the level of production that yields maximum profits. It only gives us an idea of the quantity the firm must sell so that gross profits per unit equal average fixed costs. And even then we must not lose sight of the fact that the total revenue curve in particular is difficult to estimate. Finally, this method can only be applied easily where output is homogeneous. For heterogeneous production, direct costing is the method commonly employed.

The great advantage of direct costing lies in the fact that there is no allocation of fixed costs; this in itself produces a considerable saving of labour. Where it is not so important to know the cost (because direct costing is only a partial costing method), that is, in plants that have no need to worry about profits or whose production and sales do not vary widely, this method is to be recommended. Whenever an accurate knowledge of cost is wanted (custom work or unit production), then absorption costing is indicated. However, the two methods can be combined.

In practice it is not easy to determine the optimum level of production. If we apply break-even analysis, we have to estimate future revenue, as we must with direct (standard) costing too. Pricing is therefore of the greatest importance; normally, the aim should be to maximize profits. Profit- seeking, however, is not always the primary consideration in running a business. And many entrepreneurs' decisions (like those of the consumer) are questions of pure habit. This is especially true of frequently repeated purchases and those involving a small outlay. Personal feelings and reactions play their part, too.

4. SUPPLY AND REVENUE

Like the demand curve, the supply curve is extremely difficult to construct (partly because the other things assumed to be equal do not in fact remain equal). Here, too, potential reactions will be examined over a limited price range only. Since prices are regarded as given, the supply schedule holds good only in the case of pure competition. Moreover, lags are being ignored. The elasticity of supply is even more difficult to determine than that of demand, and it has not been studied as thoroughly.

Bearing in mind the remarks on demand, we need not be surprised that the concept of the average revenue curve does not lead very far in practice. The supplier should be guided by an estimated curve and has, in fact, no concrete data to draw on in making this estimate. In view of the supplier's uncertainty, he or she should start rather from a demand or sales zone. Generally, however, the supplier does not know all these concepts. In the end, the quantities sold do not depend on price alone, and in many cases the price is not even a decisive factor. When the output of a monopolistic enterprise increases, a fall in prices is not inevitable, because in many cases we have to deal with administered prices.

5. THE INVESTMENT DECISION

Entrepreneurs often rely on methods that amount to working out the expected return on an investment. In the present value calculation and internal rate of return method, the assessment of an investment project is determined mainly by the estimated revenues and by the target rate of interest, the latter depending on both the market rate of interest and the ratio of owned to borrowed capital. The payoff method also amounts to an estimate of the rate of interest, which in most cases is high. Applied to one and the same investment project, the first two methods will produce the same result.

The difficulty lies in estimating future returns – not only their annual level but also how long they will accrue. At an interest rate of 50 percent, a four-year forecast is sufficient. Estimates that are reliable or at all accurate are generally impossible to obtain. This explains the success of the relatively simple payoff method. If, however, the entrepreneur asks too much in respect of the payoff (the period taken is too short), he or she runs the risk of lagging behind technological advance (by not proceeding to the investment). The preference for a short payoff period springs from the fact that entrepreneurs can anticipate the movement of certain factors for only a limited period.

Experience shows that the influence of the rate of interest on investment decisions, particularly the decisions of established concerns, is relatively slight. It appears to increase only when the rate is high (say, 15 percent or more). The investment programmes (and reserves) of large firms run to a number of years and are not influenced by small interest rate fluctuations.

Generally speaking, the theory being applied does not take into account the stock of capital goods. If the entrepreneur considers his or her stock of capital goods sufficient, then the entrepreneur will not invest, whatever the rate of interest. This might make us claim that there is a closer link between investment and the desired stock of capital goods than between investment and interest (a decision to invest is often made simply because it proves technically necessary): to check the accuracy of such a claim is quite a problem because the appropriate size of capital goods stocks is difficult to establish.

Other factors are of great importance to the investment decision – changes in technological knowledge, the growth rate of demand, the probable trend of costs (fluctuations in the price of production factors), the attitude of government (tax policy). One must also consider the reactions of other producers: If their market share is threatened, they too will make efforts to invest – which may result in excess capacity. The pursuit of greater power and psychological motives may also play a role.

All this shows that the entrepreneur's investment decision cannot normally be based on a few simple criteria: too many subjective elements come into play. It is unwise to cover risk by increasing the target rate of interest or reducing the payoff period without good reason; it is much more advisable to build up general reserves. For the most part, deciding what investment should be made is still what A.I. Diepenhorst calls a refined form of fortune telling.[3]

6. CONCLUSION

From what has been said it follows that the theory in application is not in line with the true facts: 'The real world still escapes our models ... we wonder whether economics can ... continue to ignore the actual decision-making processes of real firms'.[4]

Notwithstanding the important role of the entrepreneur – and the (salaried) manager is in many cases not the owner[5] – there is at the moment 'no established economic theory of the entrepreneur'.[6]

NOTES

1 J. Robinson, *The economics of imperfect competition,* 2nd ed. (London: MacMillan, 1969), p. 330.

2 Direct costs (which can be identified relatively easily with a specific unit of output) may be either fixed (the cost of a machine used to make a specific product) or variable (the cost of raw materials). Other costs are classified as indirect. Direct costing is sometimes inaccurately called marginal costing. See e.g., F.C. Lawrence and E.N. Humphreys, *Marginal costing,* 2nd ed. (London: Macdonald and Evans, 1967); J.P. de Bodt, *Critique économique du prix de revient industriel. Avec illustration concrète de l'utilisation de la méthode de la comptabilité marginale,* 2nd ed. (Louvain: Nauwelaerts, 1966).

3 A.I.Diepenhorst, quoted in H.J. Kruisinga, *Het selecteren van investeringsprojecten. Een bedrijfseconomische beschouwing van enige aspecten van het investeringsbeleid* (Leiden: Stenfert Kroese 1957), p. 23.

4 R.M. Cyert and C.L. Hedrick, Theory of the firms. Past, present and future; an interpretation, *The Journal of Economic Literature,* June 1972, p. 409.

5 Friction between managers and owners is less frequent than friction between managers and banks.

6 M. Casson, *The entrepreneur* (Oxford: Martin Robertson, 1982), p. 9.

4. THE THEORY OF PRICING

In this chapter, marginalism and two of its basic assumptions will be discussed. Finally, some comments will be made on price interdependence and the laws of supply and demand.

I. MARGINALISM

According to marginal price theory, the entrepreneur attempts to equate marginal cost and marginal revenue in order to maximize profits. However, firms actually employ other methods in pricing. In general, entrepreneurs apparently do not even know these marginal concepts.

The general use of full-cost pricing (absorption costing) – fully allocated cost plus a fixed or variable profit margin – has been illustrated by R.L. Hall, C.J. Hitch,[1] W.J. Eiteman,[2] P.J.D. Wiles[3] and B. Fog,[4] among others.

According to P.W.S. Andrews,[5] firms employ a 'normal' price. This is distinguished from absorption costing in that it takes potential competition more into account, thus restricting the opportunity for immediate profits. Potential competition can come either from new firms or from existing firms (if they convert their production facilities).[6]

The marginal method does not determine whether fixed costs, and hence average total costs, are covered. So this requires further examination. Sales promotion costs, moreover, are given little weight. While the technique proceeds as though producers and consumers were in direct contact, this is rarely the case. Frequently, it is even the wholesaler who actually sets prices. Marginal costs (especially in the long term) and above all marginal revenue cannot as a rule be calculated, and the countless attempts to determine the demand curve empirically have been unsuccessful (see Chapter 2, section 4).

One of the other objections to marginalism is that it attaches no importance to stability considerations. It assumes that changes in marginal cost and revenue are immediately reflected in changes in price. The continuous price fluctuations that result, however, encourage speculation. Both dealers and consumers prefer price stability, which also makes it easier for firms to plan ahead. In other words, it is often better to let a short-term advantage go in order to safeguard long-term interests (*inter alia* with an eye to potential competition, which may come from either new or existing firms). What are known as *administered prices* meet these requirements.

In addition, there may be objection to the marginal method on the grounds that it establishes the most profitable level of output (not price). In reality, the business executive first sets his price; only then does he or she consider what quantity it will be possible to sell. In determining this quantity, marginal theory does not even make allowance for the need to use as much as possible of the capacity available. It is in no way concerned with unused capacity (because fixed costs are not taken into account).

A detailed critique of the marginal price theory cannot be given here. (I will not engage in vague and romantic criticism, as exemplified by the remark sometimes made that marginalism would be 'antirevolutionary'.) In addition, it may be mentioned that when higher prices are ascribed to monopolistic competition and oligopoly rather than to pure competition, this applies only if the cost curves remain unchanged. Greater output, on the other hand, generally brings costs down.

Let us take oligopoly, a prevalent market structure. Following accepted hypotheses concerning both the aims of the firm concerned and its competitors' reactions, numerous divergent theories can be developed. The term *oligopoly,* in fact, covers highly divergent market situations; some oligopolies, for instance, involve three competitors, other twenty. The size of the firms may vary. Oligopolies may be homogeneous or heterogeneous, uncoordinated or coordinated. Consequently, it is not easy to formulate a general statement, and the lack of a satisfactory theory is not surprising. Hence, M. Shubik states: 'There is no oligopoly theory. There are bits and pieces of models'.[7] Oligopoly is 'the real blind spot in price theory',[8] 'a disturbing and recalcitrant problem, especially to the mathematically minded theorist, who insists upon having 'the answer',[9] and T. Seitz correctly points out that 'theoretically based statements about oligopolistic price leadership are only possible to a very limited extent'.[10]

F. Machlup, who with E. Schneider[11] is one of the most ardent advocates of the marginalist theory of the firm, finds no flaw in the marginalist tenet that the firm is 'a theoretical construct' that should not be confused with 'a real organization'.[12]

'Marginal theory of the firm', to quote Machlup again, 'should not be understood to imply anything but subjective estimates, guesses and hunches'.[13] How these are arrived at and what they really consist of, however, is not explained.[14]

The real drawbacks to the marginal theory of price, however, are the two major assumptions on which it rests; although it is mentioned incidentally that business executives can have objectives other than profit maximization, it is assumed that profit maximization is the only important aim; it is also assumed that price and quality are the business executive's chief policy instruments, even when it is admitted that he or she may sometimes have others to rely upon. We shall deal with these two assumptions in turn.

2. CORPORATE OBJECTIVES

An examination of corporate behaviour is the only means of studying how a firm reaches its decisions. Empirical studies have shown that as a general rule a variety of aims are pursued.

Among the most prominent objectives of major corporations in the United States are a satisfactory (not a maximum) revenue on investment, stable prices and profit margins, gaining or holding a given market share and meeting or forestalling competition. In Denmark the small firms appear to pursue maximization of profits in the short run while the large firms, though their aims are the same, give more attention to long-term considerations.[15] The behaviour of the small firms is due, in some cases, to a shortage of liquid assets.

W.J.Baumol regards maximizing sales as the foremost objective, at least provided total profits do not fall below a specified minimum.[16] More particularly, the aim should be maximization of the rate of growth of sales. Maximizing sales is a matter of prestige, and a firm will endeavour to preserve or increase its share of the market. At the same time, managers seek to demonstrate their ability, and this may lead to higher salaries in that company or elsewhere[17] (especially in the most common case where they hold little or none of the firm's capital). Power is often an objective, but how can we measure power?

Like the consumers, the producers try to economize on transaction costs. This can be achieved by contracts. But in doing so they impede the market. In order to cope with transaction costs firms change the corporate structure and internalize transactions.[18]

Occasionally, the main purpose of the entrepreneur is, especially in independent firms, simply a quiet life. Leisure is preferred over higher pofits (upon which higher taxes are imposed), security over more risks, good relations with colleagues over rivalry. This is by no means fanciful: The slow rate of economic growth in some countries may partly be attributed to it.

In many cases, the need for a minimum of liquid assets is in conflict with the target of maximizing profits: A firm usually tries to avoid substantial indebtedness and preserve its independence, hence the preference for self-financing. Moreover, as we have already seen, the avoidance of potential competition is incompatible with a policy directed at maximizing profits. This in fact also applies to firms wishing to maintain good relations with consumers, suppliers, investors, trade unions and above all the government.

Anyway, profit maximization cannot be regarded as the major objective of the firm; other objectives, relating to sales, production and stocks, are by no means subsidiary. The importance of these aims varies from case to case, and no general rules can be formulated here. Within the firm, the various objectives themselves often give rise to conflicts between the heads of different divisions. The determination, persuasiveness, or other qualities of one executive will sometimes turn the scales.

3. INSTRUMENTS OF CORPORATE POLICY

Although they are not the only instruments of marketing policy, almost exclusive attention is given to price and quantity in economic theory. Often, however, price is of subordinate interest, and the other policy instruments such as quality (very often closely related to R&D expenditure), sales promotion, distribution channels and product-line policy, are more important. The extent to which these different instruments (which constitute the marketing mix) are used has not yet been examined very closely. The choice of instruments depends first of all on the nature of the goods offered for sale. The financial situation may also be of great significance. There are no general rules. Time and again we see that a firm obtains better results by attaching importance to such items as advertising and packaging rather than by lowering the selling price.

a. Price

Price sensitivity varies from product to product, from consumer to consumer. There are many goods (or types of good) for which the consumer pays little attention to price; on the other hand, there are others for which price is of great significance. Consumers comparing prices (over a certain period, and at the same moment but in different shops), are less numerous than is generally supposed. Mostly, they are only informed about a limited number of prices.

Price increases are not to be condemned out of hand. They can be explained as being due to improved quality or greater demand. In certain cases (even for homogeneous goods), however, firms systematically price their products above their competitors' (this is made possible by product differentiation) to create the impression that they are offering better quality. Due to the (largely irrational) behaviour of consumers, insignificant changes are often made to a product in order to sell it at a higher price (product variation).

Price reductions are sometimes believed to signify a decline in quality, an unsuccessful line, difficulties in maintaining liquidity, or the imminent introduction of a new model. A price cut may, in fact, appreciably reduce sales of a product, when a certain class of consumers is attracted precisely because of its price.

b. Quality

This is a concept that can cover industrial design, packaging, servicing, delivery times and product variation. For many goods and services (dry cleaning, for instance) price is not as important as quality and speedy delivery. The quality of durable goods is often kept low deliberately in order to make them wear out sooner and thus promote replacement purchases. When the consumer is accustomed to a price that is a good round figure, the quality (or the weight) of a product (e.g. a bar of chocolate) is often reduced as an alternative to increasing the price (a practice known as *price line pricing*). Packaging and servicing are becoming steadily more important. This also applies to product variation. It is no simple matter to determine optimum quality and the corresponding selling price.

c. Sales promotion

Sales promotion is the practice whereby firms employ representatives and advertising to inform dealers and consumers of the qualities of their products and to encourage them to buy. The word is used in its narrower sense here, since price and quality are also means of stimulating sales.

Advertising, in addition to its useful function of providing information, can force prices up. In many cases, advertising does not increase a firm's market share because of the compensatory effect of advertising by competing firms. Firms are often put out of business by competitors whose products are inferior but who put a bigger effort into sales promotion.

d. Distribution

A firm can see to the distribution of its own products or can give the job to outsiders. Everything here depends on the consumers to be reached, the need to provide information (e.g. with consumer durables) and the type and status of the product. Prestige, for example, will probably rule out distribution through chain stores, although it must be borne in mind that these are becoming increasingly important.

The main drawback to distribution through independent retail firms, in fact, lies in the margin competition resulting from resale price maintenance – competition shifts from the consumer to the distributor. As the retailer stimulates sales of the most profitable products, the producer tends to set prices at a level that permits distribution margins at least equal to or, preferably, higher than those granted by his or her competitors. This tendency explains the possibility of 'rebate wars' (especially during a depression).

e. Product range

Industrial and, to an even greater extent, commercial firms are often constrained to increase the number of types of goods they produce – in other words, to widen their product range. This strengthens their bargaining position vis-à-vis competitors with only a few products and vis-à-vis the distributors handling their products.

4. PRICE INTERDEPENDENCE

The application of the 'theory'[19] of price interdependence has not yielded the results that were originally expected. It is no longer accepted that a system of simultaneous equations with the same number of equations as unknowns will yield an equilibrium solution (no forces at work to upset the equilibrium). Equality is neither a sufficient nor a necessary condition for the existence of a solution (even for the existence of one single solution). Attempts have accordingly been made in recent years to determine the conditions for a general equilibrium. So far, these have all been based on perfect or pure competition (and other unrealistic hypotheses, such as a constant number of economic units and goods produced, no returns to scale, no externalities, stability of the consumers' preferences, etc.). The statement of U. Ricci on the theory of general equilibrium is still valid: 'a marvellous castle . . . but of no help in solving the housing problem'.[20]

5. THE 'LAWS' OF SUPPLY AND DEMAND

The 'laws' of supply and demand are questionable as well. A variation in demand will virtually always elicit a change in supply and, conversely, a variation in supply a change in demand. Rising demand may thus be conducive to an increase in supply, where the additional output affords a reduction in the cost. In this event there is no price increase, and there may even be a reduction.

Textbooks give the impression that instantaneous adjustments occur, but they are silent as to how long it takes markets to attain equilibrium and as to what happens during the period of disequilibrium.

Thus, all possibilities are left open, and little use can be derived from the 'laws' of supply and demand. Hence, there is reinforcement for R. Harrod's contention that they will play only a minor part in the 'economics of the future'.[21] Price expectations, moreover, may lead to opposite reactions, which brings A. Lowe to the conclusion that 'such volatility of expectations . . . disconfirms the Law of Supply and Demand . . .'[22] and one can agree with G. Tarde's view that prices are determined by opinion rather than by the law of supply and demand.[23]

6. THE EFFECTS OF MARKET STRUCTURE AND CONDUCT ON PERFORMANCE

Economists try unrelentingly to find a link between market structure on the one hand and market conduct and performance on the other hand. Such a relation would be very useful in the application of competition policy. J.S. Bain did pioneering work in this respect.[24]

a. Market structure

It is difficult to make general pronouncements; divergent types of market structure yield satisfactory performance.

While monopolies and oligopolies may present many drawbacks, such as excessively high prices, profits and outlay on advertising, their inhibiting effect on technological progress, and their opposition to new market entries, they frequently offer corresponding advantages in lower prices or higher expenditure on research – and this is conducive to industrial innovation.[25]

In the United States, high concentration brings higher profits, and more so when market entry is difficult. Product differentiation also goes together with high profits, less efficient plants, and higher selling costs. According to W.G. Shepherd 'high market shares do tend to decay, but only at moderate or slow rates'.[26] But R.E. Caves believes 'better performance in some dimensions, and no worse performance in others 'would result from a reduction of concentration in manufacturing industries and lower barriers to the entry of new firms.[27]

In the European Economic Community too concentration 'does lead to higher profits and higher wages, but not to greater research efforts'. As far as 'big business' is concerned, the 'main consequence of a larger size is to reduce the variability of profit rates'.[28]

The structure of demand affects market performance. In a bilateral monopoly there is normally bargaining between the two parties, and bargaining power is of predominant significance. Compared with a monopoly, a bilateral monopoly may give a lower price level. This is also possible when a coordinated oligopsony (as in the pooling of raw-material purchases) confronts a monopoly.[29]

A weak oligopsony, however, gives rise to individual purchases, which the monopolist will turn to advantage in price discrimination. Department stores thus buy their products at lower prices than nonintegrated retailer firms. In a sellers' market the advantages of a dominant position are not always expressed in the form of lower purchase prices, but as guaranteed supplies.

When a weak oligopoly is confronted by an oligopsony, the major suppliers cannot impose their terms to the same extent as a monopolist can, since the buyers have some choice of sources of supply. Moreover, substitute products are generally available. In a market where supply is atomistic and demand concentrated, even greater pressure can be brought on prices.

b. Market conduct

Here again there is great difficulty in showing any connection with market performance. Conduct that appears to be directed at maximum joint profits in fact takes other considerations into account, such as fear of potential competition, mistrust of competitors, the possibility that less efficient firms may be better equipped on account of the high profits.

Administered prices are becoming more and more common. Product differentiation is the pre-eminent method of competition. Actual price competition is practised to some degree among department stores, but not as fully as their organization would allow.

More evidence concerning structure and performance is obtained when there is aggressive market conduct. In a price war – a rare occurrence – small competitors are sometimes squeezed out of the market and potential entrants discouraged. Identical results are obtainable by securing control of distribution channels. In such cases the market structure (greater concentration or more difficult market entry) and the market performance (prices) are directly affected by market conduct.

7. CONCLUSION

We need not be surprised that there has been much criticism of the theory of pricing. J. Robinson somewhat exaggeratedly complains that 'economic science has not yet solved its first problem – what determines the price of a commodity?'[30] The theory of pricing only provides us with '... either some common generalities ... or an abundance of complicated but useless theories ...'[31] it is 'devoid of specific substantive content'.[32] Power relationships are not taken into consideration. A.R. Oxenfeldt justifiably states: 'The detailed analysis of prices ... suggests that every price is unique in some important respect. No fairly simple explanation of price, like the law of supply and demand, has been uncovered'.[33] As K.E. Boulding puts it, 'Most people who actually set prices seem to get along very well without (the rather forbidding mass of literature known as price theory)'.[34]

Business executives who do not adhere to the rules of marginalism are no wiser as a result of the application of the full standard cost. The latter merely indicates the minimum selling price in the long run; in the short term this function is performed by the variable standard cost. It does not indicate the level at which the selling price should be set (for demand must be considered), and here, as previously shown, the producer has no firm data to go on. This explains why experts agree that setting prices is more of an art than a science. In certain cases – price discrimination or a slump – products may be sold at a loss; many factories produce different commodities to which varying margins are applied; profits are greater on one article than on another, according to the (fluctuating) potential of the market. New products especially can sometimes be priced far above cost, as was the case with the first ballpoint pens. Psychological considerations also play a part: Consumers are, for instance, more sensitive to a price increase from \$0.95 to \$1.05 than to a rise from \$0.75 to \$0.85.

Hence Austin Robinson remains 'unrepentantly of the opinion that a new attempt at understanding and presenting the processus of industrial pricing should begin afresh with a *tabula rasa* and not handicap itself with the oversimplifications of the earlier and unrefined concepts of full-cost pricing'.[35]

NOTES

1 R.L. Hall and C.J. Hitch, Price theory and business behaviour, *Oxford Economic Papers,* May 1939, reprinted in *Oxford Studies in the price mechanism* (ed. T. Wilson and P.W.S. Andrews, Oxford: Clarendon Press, 1981).

2 W.J. Eiteman, *Price determination. Business practice versus economic theory* (Ann Arbor: University of Michigan, 1949).

3 P.J.D. Wiles, *Price, cost and output* (Oxford: Basil Blackwell, 1956).

4 B. Fog, *Industrial pricing policies. An analysis of pricing policies of Danish manufacturers* (Amsterdam: North Holland, 1960).

5 P.W.S. Andrews, A reconsideration of the theory of the individual business, *Oxford Economic Papers,* Jan. 1949, p. 81.

6 P.W.S. Andrews, *Manufacturing business* (London: Macmillan, 1959), p. 176. See also

P.W.S. Andrews and E. Brunner, *Studies in pricing* (London, New York: Macmillan, 1975).

7 M. Shubik, art. cit., p. 415.

8 D.C. Hague, The task of the contemporary theory of pricing, in *Price formation in various economies. Proceedings of a conference held by the International Economic Association,* ed. D.C. Hague (London: Macmillan, 1967), p. 9.

9 E.H. Chamberlin, On the origin of oligopoly, *The Economic Journal,* June 1957, p. 218.

10 T. Seitz, *Preisführerschaft im Oligopol* (Köln: Carl Heymans, 1965), p. 241.

11 E. Schneider, Der Realismus der Marginalanalyse in der Preistheorie, *Weltwirtschaftliches Archiv,* Heft 1, 1954, reprinted in E. Schneider, *Volkswirtschaft und Betriebswirtschaft* (Tübingen: J.C.B. Mohr (Paul Siebeck), 1964).

12 F. Machlup, Theories of the firm: marginalist, behavioral, managerial, *The American Economic Review,* March 1967, p. 4.

13 F. Machlup, Marginal analysis and empirical research, *The American Economic Review,* Sept. 1946, p. 522.

14 J.L. Bouma, *Ondernemingsdoel en winst* (Leiden: Stenfert Kroese, 1966), p. 45.

15 B. Fog, op. cit., pp. 28–35.

16 W.J. Baumol, *Business behavior, value and growth* (New York: Macmillan, 1959), p. 49.

17 Cf. W.G. Lewellin, *The ownership of capital* (New York: Columbia University Press, 1971).

18 O.E. Williamson, The modern corporation. Origins, evolution, attributes, *The Journal of Economic Literature,* Dec. 1981, p. 1543.

19 Since general equilibrium theory 'has no empirical content, it is difficult to justify the very term *theory*' says M. Blaug. Its most prominent defenders have labelled it *framework* or *paradigm:* (M. Blaug, *The methodology of economics or how economists explain* (Cambridge: Cambridge University Press, 1980), p. 189.

20 U. Ricci, Pareto e l'economia pura, *Giornale degli Economisti,* Feb. 1924, p. 92.

21 R. Harrod, *Sociology, morals and mystery* (London: MacMillan, 1971), p. 76.

22 A. Lowe, op. cit., p. 48.

23 G. Tarde, *Psychologie économique* (Paris: F. Alcan, 1902), p. 176 et seq.

24 J.S. Bain, *Industrial organization,* 2nd ed. (New York: John Wiley, 1968).

25 Cf. F.M. Scherer, *Industrial market structure and economic performance,* 2nd ed. (Chicago: Rand McNally College Publishing Company, 1980), p. 266, p. 294, p. 438.

26 W.G. Shepherd, The elements and evolution of market structure; in *Markets, corporate behaviour and the state. International aspects of industrial organization,* ed. A.P. Jacquemin and H.W. de Jong (The Hague: Martinus Nijhoff, 1976), p. 211.

27 R.E. Caves, The determinants of market structure. Design for research, in *Markets, corporate behaviour and the state,* op. cit., p. 3.

28 A.P. Jacquemin and L. Phlips, Concentration, size and performance of European firms, in *Markets, corporate behaviour and the state,* op. cit., p. 74.

29 Cf. F.M. Scherer, op. cit., p. 312.

30 J. Robinson, *An essay on Marxian economics* (London: MacMillan, 1947), p. 79.

31 J. Wemelsfelder, *Onaardige economie* (Amsterdam: de Bussy, 1964), p. 191.

32 H.H. Liebhafsky, *The nature of price theory* (Homewood Ill.: Dorsey, 1968), p. 7.

33 A.R. Oxenfeldt, *Industrial pricing and market practices* (Englewood Cliffs, N.J.: PrenticeHall, 1951), p. 577.

34 K.E. Boulding, The uses of price theory, in *Models of markets* (ed. A.R. Oxenfeldt, New York: Prentice Hall, 1963), p. 146.

35 A. Robinson, Comment, in *Economics in disarray,* op. cit., p. 232.

5. THE THEORY OF INCOME DISTRIBUTION

The customary theory of distribution is greatly influenced by marginal theory. According to this theory, the first principle underlying demand for factors of production is that the factors' marginal productivities should be in proportion to the sums paid for them. In the demand for a given factor, therefore, the price of the other factors must be taken into consideration if an optimal combination of factors is to be realized.

Further, marginal costs are always compared with marginal revenue. As long as the marginal revenue yielded by the marginal production is greater than the marginal cost, it is advantageous, say, to introduce an additional quantity of capital.

The unrealistic nature of the marginal theory has already been indicated. Marginal costs and revenue are here likewise difficult to calculate. This is also the case whenever the productivity of labour and capital goods must be compared. Labour productivity is moreover linked to the nature of the capital goods at its disposal. Thus, the productivity of a worker may be low because he or she is employed in a labour-intensive industry. It is also determined by (variable and non-measurable) motivation of labour. Moreover in the production process team productivity is often more important than individual productivity.

Marginal theory assumes homogeneous units; this is true only to a minor extent of labour supply (unskilled workers). Finally, no account is taken of power relationships and traditions. The following passage deals successively with the labour market, the market for loanable funds and the distribution of national income.

1. THE LABOUR MARKET

Little help is afforded by supply-and-demand curves of the marginal theory of distribution. The explanation offered is especially weak with respect to supply. Labour is supplied until the increasing reluctance to work becomes greater than the decreasing marginal utility of the wages. One loses sight of the possibility of actual job satisfaction. At a given moment the worker prefers leisure to an increase in income and makes greater use of educational facilities. Then we have a backward sloping supply curve. In the industrialized countries the concept of 'supply' loses its significance (quite apart from the objections that have been raised in this connection regarding demand also), because the quantity offered is determined by institutional circumstances. Working hours are fixed by the government, and overtime is permitted only under certain conditions.

The competitive labour market is the exception rather than the rule. In such a market unemployment would be impossible, the unemployed being prepared to work at lower wages. But their offer would not be accepted: it would create discontent among those in work. (They have to accept lower wages too.) The unions are also opposed to lower wages, but as they often control only a small portion of the workforce, this opposition is not necessarily effective.

Regulated labour markets (by firms, employers' organizations and unions) dominate. They take the form of (internal) labour markets within the firms. After finding an entry-level job, a worker acquires his job skills through informal on-the-job training. The firm upgrades its employees (according to its needs) instead of recruiting trained labour. The existence of several internal markets explains the divergence of wage levels for the same work in the same region: access to better paid jobs in other enterprises involves entering these enterprises at a lower level.[1] Today's labour market usually displays a bilateral monopolistic character in which one or more trade unions negotiate with one or more employers' associations to fix uniform wages in each industry. To determine in advance what wages will result is not possible, since this depends on strength of character, the competence of the negotiators, their insight into the respective bargaining positions, public opinion and the entrepreneur's fear of a substitute product gaining ground in the event of a strike.

Social, political and psychological factors are becoming as important as purely economic considerations. The growth of production per employee, the cost of living and profits are, however, taken into account; the wages in key industries and the competitiveness of the economy (degree of dependence on foreign trade) also exert an influence. When negotiations between employees and employers prove fruitless, the government often feels compelled to play the role of arbitrator.

Frequently, the joint councils of government representatives, workers' and employers' organizations argue about (or decide upon) matters that are the province of parliaments. (Even in his day, Bismarck looked upon the Prussian 'Volkswirtschaftsrat' as an instrument to reduce the authority of Parliament.) This anti-democratic corporatism is often criticized.

The economics profession has for the most part ignored the 'inconsistent approaches and empirical puzzles of the labor market ... Belief in the flexible-price world of the equilibrium-price auction market remains undisturbed as if the observed problems of the labor market did not exist'.[2]

a. Wage differentials

Normally the potential to raise wages is determined by the trend of production per man-hour. Hence, in some industries it is possible for wages to rise faster. But workers in other sectors where the rate of growth of productivity is not so high, or even nonexistent (education, medical care, manual labour, theatre, restaurants, hairdressers) want to maintain existing wage differentials. This is why wages and prices in many service industries have risen so fast that they can no longer be paid (e.g. domestic staff) or that their quality suffers consequently (e.g. crowded classes, restaurants). Even the unions have little effect on the industrial structure of wage levels.

In spite of the attempts that have been made to determine the optimal wage differences scientifically, the wages structure is still governed not only by the scarcity of labour but also by habit and tradition. What A. Ross says of the United States – 'The 'national wage structure' seems to consist of little islands of rationality in a sea of anarchy'[3] – applies equally to other countries.

b. Unions and the wage level

Unions have often succeeded in obtaining increases in real wages, mainly in the concentrated sectors. The magnitude of the effects of unionism on wages 'is at contention rather than its mere existence'.[4] They may cause a decline in production and employment.

Unemployment is not a determining factor as regards wage levels in the industrialized countries, although it does influence negotiations between employers and employees. The negotiating power of the unions is, indeed, stronger in times of full employment.

Unions go on securing wage increases – often they feel obliged to do so to justify their activity – but employers do not worry about it a great deal as long as they are able to pass these increases on in the selling price (and provided the competitiveness of those countries which are dependent on exports makes this possible). Both groups often negotiate at the expense of the (less organised) consumers.

The excessive wage increases claimed by the unions (and opposed only weakly by the employers) in most countries of Western Europe have led to capital-intensive investments, inflation and more unemployment.

The conventional theory overlooks the fact that the union is not a purely economic organization. Unions sometimes oppose technical advance and prefer short-term (subsidies to coal mines) to long-term advantages.

Typical of present-day trade unionism – at least in Western Europe – is the trend towards involvement in all possible fields. On the whole, union members are far more interested in improving their own material welfare than in the ideological conflict. As a Dutch union leader put it: 'One does not become member of a trade union to be turned into a political animal by a small group of intellectuals who consider themselves the political élite'.[5] And a French union leader even believes that strikes have to be abandoned as an 'old mythology'.[6]

Meanwhile 'the problem of modelling trade union behavior has proved to be virtually intractable'[7] and '... the precise role of unions and institutions remains an open question'.[8]

2. THE MARKET FOR LOANABLE FUNDS

According to conventional theory the interest rate is mainly determined by investments and hoarding on the demand side, and by savings and (additional) money supply on the supply side. This explanation is valid only in the long run and in the absence of monopolistic tendencies and government intervention. Since in the market for loanable funds there is no question of pure competition, it is not possible to determine the interest level by means of the supply and demand curves (which imply pure competition).

Just as in the labour market, various submarkets appear; in fact, there is no such thing as *the* interest rate. Demand for liquidities depends *inter alia* upon the level of future income (e.g. from real assets) and the moment at which it becomes available, expenditure (the greater the uncertainty in this connection, the higher the demand), the expected price trends (however, the motives for holding cash balances can be so compelling that people are prepared to accept the consequences of inflation), the already acquired property and the cost of converting financial into real assets (and *vice versa*). Financial institutions continually adapt the structure of their assets to changing circumstances (prices, interest, expectations); households only do this occasionally.

The multitude and the complexity of the factors influencing demand for cash balances makes it difficult to determine such demand. The same is true for investments in securities. This involves many possibilities, and the question as to which assets are to be preferred is not easily answered, partly because future returns are difficult to estimate. Considerations regarding increased risk and the stability of the real value (avoidance of the consequences of inflation) are also relevant. Because of the difficulty of finding precise criteria, F.H. Hahn's statement is not surprising: 'It might well be argued that in situations in which rational behaviour is so difficult individuals will adopt rules of thumb'.[9]

Demand for loanable funds in order to invest in capital goods and stocks is dependent on the internal rate of return and perhaps even more on the desired stock of capital goods. The interest rate exerts only a slight influence on investment (see Chapter 3). Thus, the demand for investment purposes may rise in spite of an increase in interest if the profit expectations rise even faster. Similarly, demand may decrease notwithstanding a cut in interest.

Regarding supply, the consequences of fluctuations in interest rates are very small with respect to low and high income. In the first case, the returns are in any event of little importance, and in the second case, savings take on a residual character, regardless of the interest rate. With respect to the middle incomes, savings are normally a fixed proportion of income, which is also little influenced by changes in interest (see Chapter 2). Other considerations are sometimes weightier, such as stability of the value of the assets acquired.

Just as the money supply and liquidity preference are the most decisive elements in the money market, so are savings and investment in the capital market. Though interest appears to exert little influence on either of them, saving and investment have a greater repercussion on the level of interest.

The market for loanable funds is more flexible than the labour market, this being due to the influence of international capital movements. These prevent governments of western countries from making use of certain instruments of monetary policy: The freedom of capital movements hampers the efficacy of these measures. That general pronouncements in connection with interest are extremely difficult is a point that also holds good for these international capital movements. Capital exports to Switzerland, for example, are explained not by a higher rate of interest but by greater confidence in the Swiss currency.

As has already been stressed, it is very difficult to make comprehensive judgments on interest. However, it is going too far to say that '. . . the rate of interest can be forgotten, at least in aggregative analysis',[10] and G.L.S. Shackle is surely exaggerating when he concludes a 'survey' of the theories on interest as follows:

> It seems likely that the interest rate, or the system of rates, will continue to receive from theoreticians the homage due to a ceremonial monarch, without in fact counting for more than such a monarch in the real affairs of western nations.[11]

The theory of interest remains one of the most difficult and debatable areas of economic science:

> The theory of interest has for a long time been a weak spot in the science of economics, and the explanation and determination of the interest rate still gives rise to more disagreement among economists than any other branch of general economic theory.[12]

Although the whole range of interest rates usually moves in the same direction, this is not necessarily the case; neither do they rise or fall in the same proportion. The business cycle has an effect. In a recession, for example, the spread is greater than during a boom and the interest on the money market can even exceed that on the capital market.

The interest structure itself is not very clear: even the specialist first has to make all sorts of calculations in order to find the actual interest rates. Divergent conditions (e.g. in the case of issue or redemption of bonds), or deliberate misrepresentation (e.g. with reference to consumer credit or personal loans) mean that only the specialist is able to assess opportunities for investing in securities with real knowledge of the facts. A report by the Organization for Economic Cooperation and Development (OECD) accurately concludes: 'In the present state of affairs, the 'market process' in many countries is basically distorted by the fact that the majority concerned are unable to ascertain the real rate'.[13]

International comparison of interest rates is equally difficult since the degree of liquidity and, particularly, taxation vary from one country to another. The higher interest on bonds in continental Europe may, for example, be explained by the fact that the banks there sell directly to the individual through a chain of branches. In the United States and Britain, on the other hand, the issues are placed chiefly in the hands of the institutional investors; there are, in fact, no direct sales to households. If this is taken into account, it is questionable whether there is a great difference in the level of interest.

3. INCOME DISTRIBUTION

In a survey on personal-income-distribution theories G.S. Sahota concludes that 'the divergence of theories remains as wide as the political ideologies and social philosophies'.[14] Hence R. Kurz's contention: 'None of the traditional methods of analysis in distributional theory can explain the actual, functional, personal or socioeconomic distribution of income and wealth'.[15]

As to distributive shares, they 'are the outcome of a wide variety of forces and any theory that attempts to tackle them directly finds itself making so many heroic, simplifying assumptions that the results are simply analytical curiosities'. Hence Blaug's incomprehension of 'the obsessive preoccupation with distributive shares'.[16]

4. CONCLUSION

Even more than the theories discussed in previous chapters, the theory of income distribution is bedevilled by numerous noneconomic factors that must be considered. Up to now, attempts to integrate these factors into the theory have proved unsuccessful.

NOTES

1 D.I. Mackay, D. Boddy, J. Brack, J.A. Diack and N. Jones, *Labour markets and different employment conditions* (London: Allen and Unwin, 1971); D. Robinson, External and internal labour markets, in *Local labour markets and wages structures,* ed. D. Robinson (Farnborough: Gower, 1970).

2 L.C. Thurow, op. cit., p. 184.
3 A. Ross, *Trade union wages policy* (Berkeley: University of California Press, 1948), p. 73.
4 C.J. Parsley, Labor union effects on wage gains. A survey of recent literature, *The Journal of Economic Literature,* March 1980, p. 29.
5 H. ter Heide, *Verslag buitengewoon congres NVV* (Amsterdam: NVV, Jan. 9, 1971), p. 62.
6 N. Forestier, Edmond Maire harcèle le syndicalisme traditionnel, *Le Figaro,* 29 Oct. 1985.
7 G.E. Johnson, Economic analysis of trade unionism, *The American Economic Review,* May 1975, pp. 23–24.
8 J. Corina, *Labour market economics. A short survey of recent theory* (London: Heinemann, 1972), p. 64.
9 F.H. Hahn, Introduction, in *The theory of interest rates. Proceedings of a conference held by the International Economic Association,* ed. F.H. Hahn and F.P.R. Brechling (London: Macmillan, 1965), p. xii.
10 R. Turvey, Does the rate of interest rule the roost?, in *The theory of interest rates,* op. cit., p. 171.
11 G.L.S. Shackle, Recent theories concerning the nature and role of interest, *The Economic Journal,* June 1961, p. 252.
12 G. Haberler, *Prosperity and depression* (London: George Allen and Unwin, 1958), p. 195.
13 *Capital markets study. General report* (Paris: Organisation for Economic Cooperation and Development, 1967), p. 232.
14 G.S. Sahota, Theories of personal income distribution. A survey, *The Journal of Economic Literature,* March 1978, p. 40.
15 R. Kurz, *Verteilung, Konjunktur, Wachstum. Zur wirtschaftspolitischen Anwendbarkeit theoretischer Modelle* (Tübingen: Institut für angewandte Wirtschaftsforschung, 1982), p. 30.
16 M. Blaug, op. cit., p. 198. Concerning these simplifying assumptions see also F.H. Hahn, *The share of wages in the national income. An enquiry into the theory of distribution* (London: Weidenfeld and Nicolson, 1972), p. 162.

6. THE THEORY OF THE EQUILIBRIUM LEVEL OF NATIONAL INCOME AND OF PRICES

This chapter deals successively with the equilibrium level of national income, inflation, the quantity theory and the cash-balance theory.

I. THE EQUILIBRIUM LEVEL OF NATIONAL INCOME

According to the theory of macroeconomic equilibrium, the level of the national income[1] is determined by the link between consumption plus saving ($C + S$) and consumption plus investment ($C + I$), or between (ex ante) savings and investment.

The difficulties involved in determining the consumption, savings and investment curves have already been indicated. The process implies ex ante data that are related to expectations and intentions and which cannot be quantified. In a sense, it is assumed that we live in a world where all things can be predicted. Thus, to attempt an explanation of equilibrium level of national income on the basis of these curves offers little in the way of a solution; the shapes of the curves themselves even require an explanation.

In fact, the level of national income depends on numerous elements, such as the quantity and quality of production factors, technological progress and institutional circumstances. These elements *are* reflected in savings and investment, but not in a systematic way. In particular, the trend of national income is explained by the interaction of the investment multiplier and the accelerator. Objections are liable to be raised regarding the use of either concept.

a. The investment multiplier

The investment multiplier is difficult to determine statistically. The marginal propensity to consume is not constant; it differs from one population group to another, and the distribution of additional income is unknown. In practice, no distinction can be made between incomes that may or may not be the result of, for example, increased investment. A rise in national income is possible, moreover, without an initial increase in expenditure. This may occur as the result of a redistribution of income (at a disadvantage for those with a low marginal propensity to consume, and at an advantage for those with a high marginal propensity to consume). The multiplier can only be expressed in an economy where there is unemployment.

The (sometimes nearly negligible) results of additional investment are counteracted by a rise in imports as well as by the claims made by the government on part of the additional income (the so-called 'leaks'). Fluctuations in stocks frequently cancel out the multiplier effect.

All this also explains why it is so difficult, in practise, to fix the length to be assigned to the time units or periods in the theory. Knowledge of the production period and of the payment habits of the producers – who, moreover, may differ from industry to industry – is indeed not very accurate. (There may be a considerable difference in time from the moment the income is received to the moment it is spent.)

Particularly where the investment multiplier is applied to macroeconomic questions, the *qualitative* differences that accompany the quantitative changes are often overlooked as well as the fact that in many cases the quantitative changes are merely the result of the qualitative differences. H. Hegeland correctly draws attention to the fact:

> that the multiplier theory loses much of its relevance when applied to social aggregates and that it can be fruitfully applied chiefly to problems of microeconomics, i.e., when applied to the effects of changes in a single stream of expenditure within a limited sector of the economy.[2]

b. The accelerator

The acceleration theory is valid only while *all* machines are in use (no excess capacity), overtime is excluded, the relation between production factors cannot be altered (unchanged technology), sufficient raw materials and labour are present and the entrepreneurs command the necessary financial means. Since these conditions do not usually all exist simultaneously (the machines, for example, are usually replaced by better ones), the accelerator has minor significance; the attempts to measure the accelerator have yielded few results. This is partially due to the difficulty in distinguishing between autonomous and induced investment (particularly on the macroeconomic level).

In order to explain entrepreneurs' investment behaviour, numerous other factors must be taken into consideration. Future expectations play a particularly important part (a capacity shortage cannot be made up immediately; stocks are utilized instead). Investments are made in capital goods, not related to changes in income (e.g. under pressure of increased real wages), while autonomous investment becomes more important (new inventions, public works). The theory is based upon 'balanced' growth: Income and the stock of capital goods increase in the same proportion. This is not the case. Economic growth, furthermore, is not dependent on capital only.

As in the case of the multiplier, the pitfalls of macroeconomic data must be pointed out. A rise in investment can follow increased consumption in a given sector, while the general level of consumption can nevertheless remain the same. This investment could then erroneously be classified as *autonomous*. The accelerator, therefore, is not adequate for explaining changes in aggregate investment. Only under special circumstances and in the short term is there a proportional relationship between output and the stock of capital goods.

The acceleration principle is less general than the multiplier. Whereas the latter operates in both directions, the acceleration principle is effective only in the upward direction – and then only when the firm concerned is operating at full capacity (in the downward direction only if there is no provision for replacement investment).

c. *The interaction*

Objections can be raised regarding the use of the multiplier and the accelerator. A statistical determination of either concept is, in fact, out of the question: Neither the accelerator nor the multiplier (marginal propensity to consume) remains constant. In a recovery period, for example, the accelerator would have to be very low, since excess capacity is available; it would have to rise rapidly as soon as the economy is working at full capacity. The opposite would have to occur with respect to the multiplier.

Whenever it is logical to include the multiplier in the analysis (recovery), it is less convenient for the accelerator. In the case of full capacity operation, on the other hand, the inclusion of the accelerator in the reasoning is justified, while that of the multiplier is not.

The explanation of income fluctuations through the interaction of the multiplier and the accelerator is purely endogenous. There is doubt as to whether entrepreneurs base their long-term decisions only on short-term considerations. In most cases exogenous factors and random shocks play an important role. The influence of the monetary and financial aspects of the business cycles are mostly neglected in the many models that have been developed. A synthesis of these models is still a desideratum.[3]

d. Unemployment

A great deal of interest has been shown in the relation between, on the one hand the fluctuations of national income and the general price level, and, on the other hand, changes in unemployment.

According to A. Okun, for each three percentage points by which the annual growth rate of real output exceeds the growth rate of potential output, the unemployment rate drops by one percentage point over a period of one year.[4] But this relation presupposes a steady growth rate of productivity. Since this has not been the case Okun's Law gradually became less and less accurate and has now been dropped as a tool of analysis entirely.[5] Moreover, unemployment and employment can move in the same direction.

Another 'law' simplifying highly complex problems, is illustrated by the Phillips curve,[6] according to which full employment and a stable level of prices cannot be pursued at the same time. The Phillips relation is applicable rather to the past century and the beginning of the twentieth century than to recent decades, more to the less-developed than to the developed countries. When a relatively high unemployment percentage was accompanied by steep increases in prices (stagflation), the theory was adjusted by proceeding not from nominal but from real fluctuations in prices. Even then the lack of coherence between prices on the one hand and the unemployment percentage on the other is not explained satisfactorily. According to A. Woll, the Phillips relation has no significance in the long run, yet it may operate temporarily.[7]

2. INFLATION

The continuous overall rise in prices of consumer goods can be explained mainly by the rapid increase in the money supply. This is caused by the fact that the central bank does not (or cannot) counteract overspending (demand-pull inflation). However, this is not the only cause of inflation, as is often suggested.

Autonomous increase in wages, profits, and raw materials (which are not influenced by the former or the present level of demand) also lead to increases in costs and prices, out of which a cost-push inflation develops. Here I have in mind particularly exaggerated claims on the part of the trade unions. The cost push, however, reinforces the demand pull, and vice versa – but the two are difficult to distinguish in a period of expansion. The dangers of cost push vary from country to country, according to competitiveness. When profits provide the basis of a cost push, 'markup inflation' is the term used.

Inflation has usually been sustained by wage increases in excess of productivity growth. T. Balogh (who was one of Harold Wilson's economic advisors) is categoric on this point: 'It is clear that the inflation in the United States, as in Britain, has been caused by wages rising too fast'.[8]

The drive for higher wages is not only an expression of the union's need to justify its activity, but also of the union members' desire to satisfy greater needs. The government is asked to be more assiduous in attending to collective wants, environmental protection and full employment. This policy involves heavy spending ... and higher taxes. Everyone tries to shift these taxes on others by demanding higher (gross) incomes or by passing them on in prices. Inflation often seems to be very high in countries with a heavy fiscal burden.[9]

3. THE TRANSACTIONS EQUATION AND THE QUANTITY THEORY

a. The transactions equation of exchange

The exchange equation, $M\ V = P\ T$, needs no proof.[10] The goods are exchanged for one another: The money available is equal to the amounts needed to pay for the transactions.

The formula enables us to express any one of the factors as a function of the others ($M = P\ T/V$; $V = P\ T/M$; $P = M\ V/T$; $T = M\ V/P$), though this does not tell us anything about the factors themselves. M for instance is partly determined by the structure of the banking system, V by the way the economic units normally make payments, *P* by monopolistic conditions, and *T* by the quality and quantity of the production factors.

The time element is disregarded. Present funds are sometimes used to pay for past transactions, often at prices differing from the current ones. Moreover, *M* is a stock at a point in time (although an average can be calculated for a given period), while *T* is a flow over a period of time.

Remember, there are dangers involved in using aggregated data. Various price indices have been compiled on account of the heterogeneity of the various commodities. The 'general' level of prices does not explain the price levels of the different commodity groups, and the influence of a greater amount of money is not the same in all price categories. The equation should be written as follows:[9]

$$M\,V = p_1q_1 + p_2q_2 + p_3q_3 + \ldots + p_nq_n$$

where *n* commodity groups can be distinguished.

b. The quantity theory

The oldest and best known explanation of the value of money and the changes in that value suffers from the weakness of the exchange equation. The two must not be confused, however: The exchange equation itself is neutral and says nothing of the causal relationship between the four components. The equation is to be considered as an identity, not as a behaviour relation – two concepts that are often confused.[11]

Since moderate price fluctuations appear possible without a rise in *M*, the theory can be valid only in the long term. Some supporters of the quantity theory, however, have devoted considerable attention to the effects of short-term fluctuations in the amount of money on economic activity.

Not only can the level of absolute prices be influenced, but also the relationship between the various prices (the relative prices), without altering the general level of prices. Stability, therefore, is not necessarily a guarantee of the neutrality of money (relative prices remain unchanged).

The relationship between *M* and *P* can, naturally, best be studied when *V* and *T* are constant. Particularly since 1930, however, it has been more common for an increase in *M* not to lead to a price rise, because *V* has decreased (hoarding). A fall in *M* usually does not lead to a price cut because of the rigidity of prices. In other words, the quantity theory seems to be applicable only in the case of full employment.

The direction of causality (M is the independent variable) is usually correct, but psychological factors and autonomous changes in profits and wages can cause a rise in P to bring about an increase in M. During periods of sharp price rises (e.g. in Germany after the two world wars) confidence in the currency is lost and there is a preference for goods rather than money. By this process prices are raised again, and this causes a further increase in M. Finally, there is also the possibility of indirect action (M influences interest rates and ultimately production costs and P).

4. THE CASH-BALANCE THEORY

This theory states that the quantity of money, M, is at any given moment equal to the aggregate of cash balances held by the economic units. (For a given *period,* the *average* quantity of money equals the aggregate of *average* cash balances.) These cash balances also represent a given share, b, of the total value of goods traded so that: $M = bP\,T$.

As was the case with the transactions equation of exchange, the cash-balance equation expresses an evident truth: The value of the supply of money is equal to the value of the goods for which purchasing power is retained in the form of money.

While in the transactions equation of exchange one pays attention exclusively to that portion of the amount of money destined for current transactions, in the cash-balance equation one pays attention mainly to that part retained for unforeseen expenditure. And V or b is different for each part – rather stable for the first but not for the second (under the influence of hoarding and dishoarding).

Stressing the connection between b and income actually fits in better with modern theory. The objections to the quantity theory, however, remain valid. The cash-balance theory is likewise a monetary approach to the explanation of the variations in economic life. For this purpose, both theories are based on the fluctuations, of $M\,V$ and M/b respectively. In expenditure analysis, on the other hand, changes in economic activity are explained by means of consumption and investment decisions – that is, by the fluctuations of $C + I$ (but $C + I$ and $M\,V$ are not equivalent: $C + I$ only consists of expenditure for finished products, whereas $M\,V$ comprises all payments for production factors and semifinished products too and is therefore larger than $C + I$). Depending on the approach adopted, the government uses different instruments of economic policy: on the one hand monetary policy, and on the other, control of the circular flow.

The quantity theory and the cash-balance theory are too limited as general analytical tools, though they may provide useful indications. It must be remembered that the equations concerned 'are nothing more or less than shorthand expressions designed to indicate the nature of the variables whose operations can be shown to influence prices',[12] and that these variables have still to be thoroughly investigated. Psychological factors are of great importance here: 'It appears difficult to arrive at a full understanding of fluctuations in the value of money ... without taking qualitative considerations and psychological analyses into account'.[13]

5. CONCLUSION

Once more, we must conclude that the theories considered give only partial explanations. Furthermore, there is not the slightest unanimity of opinion concerning the analysis of either the general level of income or that of prices.

NOTES

1 We shall not dwell upon the unending stream of studies on the paternity and the interpretation of Say's law: T. Sowell, *Say's law* (Princeton: Princeton Univ. Press, 1972); W.H. Hutt, *A rehabilitation of Say's law* (Athens: Ohio University Press, 1974); W.O. Thweatt, Early formulators of Say's law, *The Quarterly Review of Economics and Business,* Winter 1979.

2 H. Hegeland, *The multiplier theory* (Lund: C.W.K. Gleerup, 1954), p. 252.

3 V. Zarnowitz, Recent work on business cycles in historical perspective: a review of theories and evidence, *The Journal of Economic Lierature,* June 1985, p. 571.

4 A.M. Okun, *Prices and quantities. A macroeconomic analysis* (Washington DC: Brookings Institution, 1981).

5 L.C. Thurow, op. cit., p. 9.

6 A.W. Phillips, The relationship between unemployment and the rate of change of money wage rates in the United Kingdom 1861–1957, *Economica,* Nov. 1958.

7 A. Woll, Das Phillips-Theorem. Eine empirische Studie zum Zielkonflikt zwischen Vollbeschäftigung und Preisniveaustabilität in der Bundesrepublik Deutschland 1952–1972, in *Studien zum Inflationsproblem,* ed. T. Pütz (Berlin: Duncker and Humboldt, 1975), p. 140.

8 T. Balogh, *Labour and inflation* (London: Fabian Society, Oct. 1970), p. 22.

9 Cf. A.T. Peacock and M. Ricketts, The growth of the public sector and inflation, in *The political economy of inflation,* ed. F. Hirsch and J.H. Goldthorpe (London: Martin Robertson, 1978).

10 M: money supply; V: velocity of circulation of money; P: general price level; T: quantities traded; p: prices (sequences: $p_1, p_2 \ldots p_n$); q: quantities (sequences: $q_1, q_2 \ldots q_n$).
11 K. Klappholz and E.J. Mishan, Identities in economic models, *Economica,* May 1962, p. 117.
12 A.W. Marget, *The theory of prices. A re-examination of the central problems of monetary theory,* part 1 (Englewood Cliffs, N.J.: Prentice Hall, 1938), p. 54.
13 A. Aftalion, *Monnaie, prix et change,* 3d ed. (Paris: Sirey, 1950), p. 554.

7. THE THEORY OF ECONOMIC GROWTH

As a rule, economic growth is not measured against production capacity, which is very difficult to estimate, but against national production. In this chapter, we define economic growth as a sustained increase in the net real national product (or income) per inhabitant.

Since it is impossible to dwell on all possible theories, we shall examine only the Harrod-Domar theory, the neoclassical theory and W. Rostow's theory. We shall also deal with the factors of economic growth. Furthermore, we shall ignore the question of whether economic growth is desirable in the long run. Some authors, indeed, are fundamentally against economic growth. The antropocentric – and unscientific – basis on which the theory of economic growth proceeds is, according to J.H. Culbertson, a consequence of the 'Judeo-Christian belief, the idea that the universe was built to serve man, as a means to his ultimate exaltation'.[1] According to the same author, earlier civilisations perished because of overpopulation and pollution.

Since conventional wisdom praises the beneficial role of foreign aid for the development process in the less-developed countries, we will examine more amply the connection between aid and growth.

I. THE HARROD-DOMAR THEORY

According to this theory,[2] the relative change in the national income (g) is determined by the ratio between the propensity to save (s) and the capital-output ratio (k) as follows: $g = s/k$.

Similar to the transactions equation of exchange, this formula gives the factors that are relevant to an analysis, but it tells us nothing about the factors themselves.

The theory is based on unrealistic assumptions. The capital-output ratio does not remain constant. Authors who consider it an acceptable working hypothesis to regard the capital-output ratio as constant, are relying on excessively limited material. Insofar as reliable data are available (the calculation of macroeconomic capital is quite a feat), the ratio (as well as a change in the ratio) differs from country to country. Special circumstances repeatedly play a role. Technological progress is frequently embodied in the formation of capital, so that production is compared not only with capital but also with the technological progress embodied in capital goods. If this technological progress is not maintained, then the capital-output ratio will be too low in the next period. According to P. Streeten, 'the capital-output ratio can be of no assistance to the planner in deciding where, when, how and how much to invest'.[3]

Normally, a difference in growth between labour and capital provokes substitution phenomena. This substitution is considered impossible in the Harrod-Domar theory, where the growth rate of the national product is identical to that of the capital goods stock. This is more a short-term hypothesis rather than long term.

It is surprising that the Harrod-Domar theory does not try to show a link between an increase in the exogenously determined total or active population and the increase in the derived demand for labour that results from the increase in the stock of capital goods (labour and capital are assumed to be in a fixed ratio to each other).

A similar observation may be made about the propensity to save. Some authors, including N. Kaldor[4] and J. Robinson[5], think that, for instance, the propensity to save differs in the case of income from employment and income from entrepreneurship.

2. THE NEOCLASSICAL THEORY

Neoclassical theory assumes two production factors, perfect substitutability and flexible prices. It is also based on a constant propensity to save, but it does not assume a fixed capital-output ratio.

It must be again stressed that the propensity to save is not constant. Many prices and wages are rigid; to assume flexible prices and wages is therefore unrealistic (unemployment is not absorbed when wages fall). The ratio between capital and labour has not been fixed once and for all, and perfect substitutability is not possible either. While the Harrod-Domar theory is a macroeconomic theory, the neoclassical theory is fundamentally microeconomic.

3. W. ROSTOW'S THEORY

Rostow's thesis[6] does not concur with the statistical material available. The process of growth and the trend of investment are gradual: They do not advance by fits and starts. The industrial 'revolution' in England 'was the cumulation of a four-century period of advance in techniques'.[7] It is not clear what criteria can be used in order to distinguish one stage from another. How the 'reactive nationalism', a characteristic of the takeoff, must be interpreted, is not clear. Nor is it possible to establish in advance what industries should provide the thrust to set off economic growth. While in most cases agricultural development precedes growth in the industrial sector, the two frequently go hand in hand.

Rostow's scheme fails to take into account the fact that the less-developed countries can now avail themselves of Western experts and up-to-date equipment and thus avoid not a little trial and error and misdirected investment. They experience difficulties in exporting, however, because competition having increased in the meantime importers expect higher standards of quality and lower prices than, for instance, at the beginning of the nineteenth century, when Britain was the only exporter on an international scale.

Rostow has the merit of not wanting to give a purely economic theory of economic growth. However, some of his statements concerning the link between economics and politics are at least susceptible to criticism (e.g. when he says that industrialization goes together with the pursuit of democracy).

4. THE FACTORS OF ECONOMIC GROWTH

Numerous growth theories, three of which have been dealt with, are based on very few (in most cases only one or two) determining elements.

Of the many factors that are of importance to economic growth, besides the institutional, political and social circumstances under which production takes place, particular mention must be made of population, natural resources, capital, education and technological progress.

a. Population

No connection exists between the growth rate of the national product and that of the population. Although demographic expansion can contribute to economic growth by inducing new investment, it acts rather as a brake when the growth of population does not give rise to an increase in demand. This is the case in most of the less-developed countries. The developed countries could provide material assistance in the efforts being made to introduce birth control in the less-developed countries: 'The modest contributions that rich countries might make to facilitate this crucial part of the modernization process could well count for more than all they are prepared to do in the realm of conventional aid'.[8]

b. Natural conditions

It is difficult to generalize regarding the connection between soil conditions or mineral resources and economic growth. The possession of rich ore deposits is not a sufficient condition for economic development (a certain monopoly power is required, e.g. petroleum), nor is the lack of them any hindrance (e.g. Japan): The extension of transport facilities, in particular, has incurred cheapness in the shipment of raw materials. Whereas in some countries with abundant natural resources the average national income shows no increase (e.g. Zaire), countries not so well off in this respect have shown steady progress.

c. Capital

Economic growth generally accompanies an increase in the importance of industry (to the detriment of agriculture). Hence the industrialisation policy of less-developed countries. Theoretically, preference should be given to investment in as many industries as possible. There are risks involved in capital investment in only one industry; income must also be raised elsewhere to absorb that industry's increased production. A big push is advised, then, to achieve balanced growth. In fact, balanced growth cannot be realized because there are insufficient financial means and a scarcity of entrepreneurs; and in some cases it would thwart the international division of labour. Some authors, including A.O. Hirschman,[9] even advocate deliberately unbalanced growth.

An increase in investment in the less-developed countries is only possible where there is efficient management and skilled labour – factors that are not normally available. Hence the importance of education and technical assistance. But there are too many lawyers and too few engineers in the less-developed countries, and primary and secondary education are often neglected in favour of higher education, so that the number of university graduates exceeds the number of openings for them.

d. Education

I. Fisher[10] already pointed out that people were to be considered as 'human capital', and expenditure on education as investment in these people (A. Marshall did not agree).[11] Since T.W. Schultz defended this proposition in 1960,[12] many economists have been advocates of the 'human capital approach'.

Apart from the difficulties involved in measuring the quality of human capital, the fact that education is not only an investment but also a consumption is overlooked. Not all education has economic purposes (e.g. history of art).

Although educational distribution has narrowed, it has had no influence on the distribution of earnings. More human capital has not given rise to productivity growth. Moreover, income is not determined solely by productivity. In fact, 'the attempt to remove the distinction between labor and other factors of production yielded some insights, but in the end the enterprise obscured more real problems than it clarified'.[13]

Both education and scientific research are of importance to economic growth, but to establish a simple connection between the two factors and economic growth is not easy.

e. Technological advance

According to R. Solow,[14] technological advance accounted for 85 percent of the growth in the American economy (national income per employee) between 1909 and 1945. E.F. Denison[15] quotes 62 percent for the United States in the period 1950–62 and 80 percent for Northwestern Europe (where the highest figure for any one country was 86 percent for Western Germany). Total productivity fell from 1.99 per cent for 1948–73 to −0.32 per cent for 1973–81. According to E. Denison 'advances in knowledge and miscellaneous determinants' are responsible for this decrease[16] ... although the amounts devoted to technical progress did not decrease. J. Kendrick obtains a positive figure for technical advance for the period 1973–78.[17] Denison's negative figure has therefore to be attributed to 'miscellaneous determinants'.

However, for the authors mentioned 'technical advance' is a broader concept. It is not a consequence of microeconomic innovation, but a macroeconomic residual factor. That part of the growth rate of the national product which cannot be explained by the increase in labour and capital is attributed to technological advance – not only technological advance in the strict sense but also improvement in the quality of production factors (e.g. a higher standard of education) and the way in which factors are combined to make for efficient product (e.g. more efficient management, economies of scale, external economies). The sum of these changes entails increased production per unit of input. Thus, the national income rises because there are changes in factor inputs and because output per unit of input increases (i.e. technological advance in the broader sense). It would be preferable to speak of production per unit of input to avoid confusion with technological advance proper.

A number of theories have been proclaimed concerning the role of technological advance in economic growth. R. Solow,[18] for instance, holds that technological advance is reflected in or is incorporated in the investment of the current year ('the latest vintage of capital'). Others remark that technological advance need not necessarily be embodied in labour or capital but should rather be considered a third production factor. K. Arrow[19] sees technological advance as a consequence rather than as a cause of economic growth.

In neoclassical theory, technological advance is considered an exogenous factor. This is one-sided point of view. Technological advance may also be the result of expenditure on education or research, in which case it is of an endogenous character, and cannot be a residual factor. The rough estimates of this residual factor and its components (e.g. education, economies of scale) could just as well be replaced by other, quite different, estimates. The hypotheses (e.g. pure competition) on which the method is based are indeed very unrealistic. Technological advance has without question been important in economic growth, but it is impossible to ascertain exactly to what extent the one accounts for the other. Whether technological advance is capital saving or labour saving (or neutral) is again very difficult to say. (An innovation may be labour saving, but it may raise the relative wage level.)

5. FOREIGN AID AND GROWTH

Foreign aid to less-developed countries is generally justified by welfare economics: it is felt intuitively that this assistance results in more utility for the less-developed countries than in disutility for the more developed.[20] We return to the limited significance of welfare economics in Chapter 10. Yet the necessity of aid-giving seems to be part of the conventional economic wisdom.

But there is a growing disenchantement with the role of foreign aid in development. Foreign aid is becoming synonymous with dissipation and corruption. In the less-developed countries there is even a nostalgia for the colonial period. According to Marx the British rule was on balance favourable to India.[21] And J. Robinson adds: 'the misery of being exploited by capitalists is nothing compared to the misery of not being exploited at all'.[22] Indeed, decolonization has been a catastrophe. Only one tenth of the roads of the former Belgian Congo can now be used. Foreign aid often serves to acquire arms in order to persecute ethnic minorities or to cover deficits due to the inefficiency and irresponsibility of the governments. The purpose is oppression and agression, rather than genuine defence. Tribal wars in Nigeria caused a million dead, in Uganda 100 000 to 300 000, in Burundi 200 000 and in Rwanda 200 000.

Foreign assistance is not necessary to economic growth, as the cases of the United Kingdom, Japan, Mexico and South Korea prove. There is no correlation between economic growth and foreign aid. Even the Development Council of the Organisation for Economic Cooperation and Development admits that foreign aid has not brought about a rise in economic growth. There is no progress in India, in spite of substantial aid. Sometimes foreign assistance is compared to Marshall aid. But the purpose of the postwar American initiative was to compensate material losses. The other ingredients of economic growth were available (which is not the case in the less-developed countries). We are not even certain that the growth rate would have been lower without Marshall aid: there was more progress in Germany with little aid than in the United Kingdom with substantial aid.

It is often alleged that foreign aid is in the interest of the donor countries. But 'none of the arguments from the selfinterest of the advanced countries – political, military, and economic – that had been used from time to time in support of official aid-giving was at all persuasive'[23] and P.T. Bauer is still more explicit: 'To argue that aid helps the domestic economy is like saying that a shop-keeper benefits from having his cash register burgled so long as the burglar spends part of the proceeds in his shop'.[24]

Foreign aid is frequently inefficient. Although it is normal for donor countries to expect the recipient of assistance to aim at non-reliance on gifts, this is generally not done. The standard of living in many less-developed countries is lower than twenty years ago[25] and according to R. McNamara the average African is poorer than in 1970.[26] The causes of the fiasco are known: population pressure (in Africa a 'real' man has many children), religion (sacred cows), instability and corruption of governments.

Moreover, Soviet-type economies preclude initiatives which lead to economic growth. 'A major cause of the distorted policy environment in many of the African nations has been the encroachment of the state into almost every sphere of economic activity . . . the control of the political elite . . . has led to the practice of accumulating wealth through access to state power rather than through contributions to productive enterprise'.[27]

Since countries which favour private entrepreneurial activity usually reach higher rates of growth and productivity increase than countries with comprehensive planning[28] it has often been proposed that aid should be given to only those countries with economic systems which favour free enterprise.

Foreign aid can even be harmful. It contributes to the creation of inefficient enterprises (e.g. state oil refineries in India), it consolidates corrupt governments and it promotes state interference. Why should governments in less-developed countries create a favourable economic climate conducive to private investments if they receive finance anyway? Training students from less-developed countries in the western countries may be beneficial to the students but not to their countries, since these students try normally to stay abroad.

American grain shipments to India have been harmful to Indian agriculture. Similar consequences have been experienced in Africa. 'Tanzania is a striking example of the effects of international wealth transfers through multilateral agencies. It has received more 'foreign aid' per capita than any other nation. Its output per worker has *declined* 50 per cent over a period of a decade; it has turned from an exporter of maize to an importer'.[29] Hunger in Africa is almost entirely the fault of the governments concerned. Chad alone could provide the entire Sahel population with food. The aid to hungry Africa is not precisely a theme for a *vaudeville* but it contains enough material for a succesful satirical drama. The numerous international organizations are fighting in vain for being entrusted the coordination of aid. The same battle for coordination of aid distribution is being waged between the various ministries in the recipient countries. But no matter who is responsible for the distribution, a great deal of the aid 'disappears'. It certainly does not reach the 'rebel' regions (e.g. Tigre and Eritrea in Ethiopia). The lack of coordination in the West is evidenced by the large number of missions sent to the less developed countries (where one mission would be sufficient). In 1981, a total of 340 missions visited Burkina Faso and the officials of that country had to give the same explanation 340 times. No wonder that the term 'development aid tourism' has found acceptance.

Without the so-called development aid, people in the third world would be better-off, says the German politician Brigitte Erler (socialist party) in a recent book, whose title is certainly not obscure: 'Deadly aid'. Food aid obstructs the development of domestic agriculture.[30]

Foreign assistance has disincentive effects on indigeneous commitments and efforts devoted to development. There is a negative correlation between foreign aid and domestic savings. This assistance does not even succeed in promoting human rights. In the Lomé Convention the EEC countries could not obtain from the ACP countries a declaration in favour of human rights.

In fact, domestic policies hold the key to the less-developed countries' performance. Some international institutions lay stress on this point: 'those Latin American countries whose residents have been exporting capital on a massive scale would be well advised to put their house in order so as to end this capital outflow and even, hopefully, to draw some of the flight capital back. It is too much to expect the rest of the world – whether multilateral institutions, governments, banks or corporations – to perform the development functions that these countries' own nationals refuse to assume'.[31] 'Corruption is on such a scale that it has major economic consequences: it may stimulate the illegal export of capital or result in large projects being awarded to contractors (often multinational companies) according to the size of their bribes rather than the quality of their performance'.[32] T. Sowell also points out that '. . . a substantial part of the current efforts of the rulers and governments of such countries often consists of repressing, impeding, or even driving out of the country those who possess the human capital to develop it'.[33]

The necessity for more cooperation between the less-developed countries only evokes a few vague statements. Time and again, UNCTAD publications maintain that closer economic cooperation between less-developed countries is the essence of a new international economic order. Since their surplus of products intended for export cannot be absorbed by the industralized nations, the less-developed countries must look more to one another for markets and for sources of supply.

Plans, agreements and conferences on regional integration have certainly not been found to be wanting either in Africa or in Latin America; to date, however, concrete results have been very few. The 'colonial' frontiers have hardly been altered, which accounts for the existence in Africa of a large number of economically unviable miniature states. All are agreed that a political rearrangement is necessary; not one head of state, however, will even consider giving up his office.[34]

Foreign aid can be justified on moral grounds but in that case it is the concern of the individual, not of the state. It is then a voluntary action (the Church admits priority of one's own family and country). Control may not be useless. In many cases only 20 percent of the funds collected by humanitarian organizations reach their destination, the rest being absorbed by administrative costs.

Since foreign aid is not a precondition for economic growth the paeans which it evokes require an explanation. In conformity with economic theory, the laudation emanates from those persons and institutions who have an interest in the preservation and augmentation of foreign assistance.

First, there are the exporters to the less-developed countries and the 'development experts' in the ministries. Especially experts writing learned reports on development for international institutions hope that development assistance will be perpetuated.

Secondly, we have the politicians in both developed and less-developed countries. Each minister of development assistance tries to demonstrate his own and his civil servants' usefulness.

Thirdly, banks in trouble that have provided loans to less-developed countries turn to the state and/or to international organizations, such as the IMF, for a helping hand. The more the less-developed countries get assistance, the greater is the chance that the banks will be reimbursed. Hence their call for more aid from the IMF and the World Bank. But neither the states nor the international institutions have to bear the risks that the banks have assumed. Some banks even blame their governments for not having prevented them from lending too much. This does not make sense. According to Sir Geoffrey Howe, the then British Chancellor of the Exchequer, this means that governments have a better view of the risks; experience shows that this is not the case. His conclusion is clear: '... countries with excessive debts must like the rest of us follow appropriate adjustments policies, and private sector banks will need to show a matching responsibility'.[35] The fourth group consists of the international institutions. Many international civil servants live on development assistance. In the OECD, the United Nations (New York, Geneva, etc.) UNCTAD, UNIDO, numerous civil servants comment on the same statistics and write the same unreadable reports. The number of these reports is actually creating storage problems (cf. the flood of UNCTAD publications). FAO spends two-thirds of its resources in Rome. The international institutions always find resources for a press that is prepared to praise their usefulness. They always find experts to prove that foreign aid is indispensable (cf. the Pearson report).

Even authors who have time and again favoured ever-increasing foreign assistance have changed their views: '... I gave unqualified support to the idea that the developed countries should give financial assistance for their (underdeveloped countries) development ... Recent happenings in the underdeveloped countries and in the world at large, however, have caused me to doubt whether I was right'.[36]

6. CONCLUSION

Economic growth is a difficult and complicated matter. John H. Adler quite accurately points out that:

> the experience of the postwar period shows the complexity and many-sidedness of the process of economic development, on the one hand, and how little we know and how much we still have to learn about it, on the other.[37]

It should not surprise us that 'we seem as far from a *general* theory as ever'.[38] Fifteen years later the same complaint is heard: 'Our knowledge about the causes of growth is still inchoate and unreliable'.[39]

The significance of each growth factor differs from country to country – the institutional circumstances in particular. This applies especially to the less-developed countries. It is a fact that there are relatively few features common to the economies of these countries: small stock of capital goods and little technological knowhow, few good entrepreneurs or managers. And there are great differences in natural resources, institutional circumstances and population. It stands to reason that economic policy in a densely populated country (with substantial disguised unemployment) will differ from that in a thinly populated country. Differences in performance are mainly due to divergent 'political organization and ... administrative competence of government'.[40]

A theory that will serve for one particular country or group of countries is not necessarily applicable to another. India, for instance, is often regarded (wrongly) as *the* example of a less-developed country. In view of this misconception, more attention is now paid to a classification of the different countries – with a theory for each type. There is no need to look for a special development theory for the less-developed countries. Attempts made along these lines have had few results. With the exception of W.W. Rostow's theory we have been offered only partial explanations. The economic dualism assumed by some authors, for instance (coexistence of a relatively small, modern, capital-intensive sector and a traditional, mainly agricultural sector), can be found in developed countries too, though to a lesser extent.

All this explains the opinion of Sir John Hicks:

> No attempt is made to present a Theory of Economic Growth ... which is to be defended as the theory superior in every respect, or even in every important respect, to any other. I do not think that there is such a theory; I much doubt if there can be![41]

NOTES

1 J.M. Culbertson, *Economic development: an ecological approach* (New York: Philadelphia Book Co, 1971), p. 294. See also F. Hirsch, *Social limits to growth* (London: Routledge and Kegan, 1971).

2 R.F. Harrod, *Towards a dynamic economics. Some recent developments of economic theory and their application to policy* (London: MacMillan, 1948); id., *Economic essays* (London: MacMillan, 1952), essay 14; id., Second essay in dynamic theory, *The Economic*

Journal, June 1960; id., Are monetary and fiscal policies enough?, *The Economic Journal,* Dec. 1964. His last work, *Economic dynamics* (London: MacMillan, 1973), requires previous reading of his 1948 work. E.D. Domar, *Essays in the theory of economic growth* (New York: Oxford University Press, 1957).

3 P. Streeten, *The frontiers of development studies* (London: MacMillan, 1972), p. 107.

4 N. Kaldor, Alternative theories of distribution, *The Review of Economic Studies,* 1956.

5 J. Robinson, *The accumulation of capital* (London: MacMillan, 1956).

6 W.W. Rostow, *The stages of economic growth. A non-communist manifesto,* 2nd ed. (Cambridge University Press, 1960); id. *Politics and the stages of growth* (Cambridge: Cambridge University Press, 1971).

7 E.E. Hagen, *The economics of development* (Homewood Ill.: Richard D. Irwin, 1968), p. 32.

8 G. Ohlin, *Population control and economic development* (Paris: OECD, 1967), p. 131.

9 A.O. Hirschman, *The strategy of economic development* (New Haven: Yale University Press, 1958), Chap. 3–4.

10 I. Fisher, *The nature of capital and income* (New York: Augustus Kelley, 1906), p. 53.

11 A Marshall, *Principles of economics,* 8th ed. (London: MacMillan, 1920), p. 650.

12 T.W. Schultz, *Education and economic growth, in Social forces influencing American education,* ed. N.B. Henry (Chicago: University of Chicago Press, 1961).

13 L.C. Thurow, op. cit., p. 180.

14 R. Solow, *Capital theory and the rate of return* (Amsterdam: North Holland, 1963), p. 96.

15 E.F. Denison, *Why growth rates differ. Postwar experience in nine western countries* (Washington: The Brookings Institution, 1967), Chap. 21.

16 E.F. Denison, Accounting for slower economic growth: An update, in *International comparisons of productivity and causes of the slowdown,* ed. W. Kendrick (Cambridge, Mass.: Ballinger Publishing Company, 1984), p. 4–5.

17 J. Kendrick, Why productivity growth rates change and differ, in *Towards an explanation of economic growth. Symposium 1980,* ed. H. Giersch (Tübingen: Mohr (Paul Siebeck), 1981), p. 121–122.

18 R. Solow, op. cit., pp. 42–43.

19 K. Arrow, The economic implications of 'learning by doing', *The Review of Economic Studies.* June 1972.

20 See, for example, Organisation for Economic Cooperation and Development, *Development cooperation. 1980 review* (Paris, 1980), p. 63–66.

21 Quoted in C. Rangel, *L'Occident et le tiers-monde* (Paris: Laffont, 1982), p. 71.

22 J. Robinson, *Economic philosophy* (London: Watts, 1962), p. 45.

23 H.G. Johnson, *Economic policies towards less developed countries* (London: Allen and Unwin, 1967), p. 53.

24 P.T. Bauer, *Equality, the Third World and economic delusion* (London: Weidenfeld and Nicolson, 1981), p. 293.

25 *Europa van Morgen,* 9 mei 1984, p. 310.

26 R.S. McNamara, *The Challenge to Sub Saharan Africa,* Sir John Crawford Memorial Lecture, Washington, 1 Nov. 1985.

27 R.S. McNamara, op. cit., p. 5.

28 E. Görgens, Entwicklungshilfe als Wachstumsmotor? Zu den Erfolgsaussichten neuerer Vorschläge zur Entwicklungshilfe im Lichte empirischen Erfahrungen, *ORDO. Jahrbuch für die Ordnung von Wirtschaft und Gesellschaft,* 1985, p. 131–152.

29 T. Sowell, *The economics and politics of race* (New York: William Marrow, 1983), p. 240.

30 B. Erler, Tödliche Hilfe. *Bericht von meiner letzten Dienstreise in Sachen Entwicklungshilfe* (Freiburg i. Br.: Dreisam-Verlag, 1985), p. 0.
31 Bank for International Settlements, *54th Annual Report* (Basel, 1984), p. 171.
32 International Bank for Reconstruction and Development, *Annual report 1983* (Washington, 1983), p. 17.
33 T. Sowell, *The economics and politics of race,* op. cit., p. 235.
34 M.A.G. van Meerhaeghe, *International economic institutions,* 4th ed. (The Hague: Martinus Nijhoff, 1985), p. 162.
35 Sir Geoffrey Howe, at the annual meeting of the IMF in Toronto, Sept. 1982. See The International Monetary Fund: its role in the world's economies, *Economic Progress Report, Supplement,* Febr. 1983, pp. 3–4.
36 G. Myrdal, International inequality and foreign aid in retrospect, in *Pioneers in development,* ed. G.M. Meier and D. Seers (New York: Oxford Press, 1984), p. 151.
37 J.H. Adler, Poverty amidst wealth: trends in the world's economy, *Finance and Development,* no. 4 (1968), p. 32.
38 B. Higgins, *Economic development. Principles, problems and policies,* rev. ed. (New York: W.W. Norton, 1968), p. 843.
39 M. Abramovitz in a book review, *The Journal of Economic Literature,* March 1983, p. 113.
40 L.G. Reynolds, The spread of economic growth to the Third World: 1856–1980, *The Journal of Economic Literature,* Sept. 1983, p. 976.
41 J. Hicks, *Capital and growth* (Oxford: Clarendon Press, 1965), p. V.

8. THE THEORY OF INTERNATIONAL TRADE

In this chapter, we will discuss the theory of comparative cost, the Heckscher-Ohlin theory, the theory of purchasing-power parity and the modern theory of balance-of-payments equilibrium.

I. THE THEORY OF COMPARATIVE COST

According to this theory, it is not the absolute but the comparative cost (which depends solely on the input of labour) that constitutes the decisive factor in determining which goods are traded with other countries. Even if a country were able to manufacture everything more inexpensively than any other country, it would be to its advantage to concentrate on producing the most profitable commodities and leave the less profitable goods to other countries.

However, the assumptions on which the theory proceeds have no factual basis. For example, costs are not due to labour alone. Moreover, labour is not homogeneous. Furthermore, there are transport costs, and the higher these costs, the less the advantage that divergent comparative costs will yield. In reality, calculations are not made with costs in kind, but with currency units. Therefore, the concept of 'opportunity cost', or 'substitution cost',[1] introduced by G. Haberler offers no solution, since here again, they are expressed in real units (i.e. the amount of the one commodity that has to be sacrificed in order to increase the production of another commodity by one unit).

While the theory tells us within what limits the exchange ratio must lie, it gives no indications as to the actual ratio, nor as to the quantities traded. This is because it disregards the importance of demand. At a later date, attempts were made – notably by J.S. Mill[2] – to take account of demand, but here too the initial assumptions were unrealistic.

Since it was from the theory of comparative cost that the need for international division of labour and free trade was derived, it was not surprising that protectionism was invoked because certain hypotheses in the theory (e.g. full employment, constant costs) were inconsistent with the hard facts: '...

protectionism (is) rather a defensive reflex than a doctrinal and aggressive tendency, more or less justified according to the case, in the face of certain fundamental problems not dealt with by classical theory.'[3]

Comparative costs, moreover, do not account *per se* for the development of trade: they themselves have to be explained.

While the individual indifference curve is open to criticism (Chapter 2), the community curve largely used in the theory of international trade is even more vulnerable. The interpersonal comparison of utility embodied in these curves is difficult to uphold. Their use implies that their form is unaffected by administrative measures, which is not in fact the case. Increased customs duties, for instance, cause the distribution of income to change. Consequently it is not surprising that '. . . it seems that those who use community indifference curves and Marshall's reciprocal demand curves have been led to formulate sweeping and positive conclusions which their underlying methodology cannot support',[4] that 'the theory of the indifference curve has not been able to solve the problems that are involved with the pure theory of international trade',[5] or 'that the use of indifference curves should be termed a dangerous matter, of dubious scientific value'.[6]

These objections[7] have led us to eschew any use of this technique 'however unrealistic', in our analysis of international trade.[8] Many other economists continue to employ it. Kindleberger, for example, excuses his use of it on the grounds that 'the community indifference curve is schematically a neat device'.[9]

2. THE THEORY OF RECIPROCAL DEMAND

J.S. Mill[10] considered that exchange must occur at a ratio at which the two quantities are identical. In other words, although he did not use the term, the elasticity of each country's demand for the other's export commodities must be taken into account. This theory was later expressed in graph form with the aid of the reciprocal demand curves developed by F. Edgeworth[11] and Marshall.[12]

Here too a number of unrealistic assumptions are adopted. Costs are again stated in kind, and while the quantities of production factors may be in equilibrium this is no guarantee of equilibrium in monetary units. No account is taken of (domestic) demand for national output. As Viner has pointed out,[13] a country would export only after satisfying home demand.

The analysis is valid only for countries where resources are approximately equivalent. A small country will often adopt the cost ratios of its larger partner. No allowance is made for fluctuations in incomes.

Graham[14] considers that the application of the reciprocal demand curves makes it appear that demand alone is of interest. He states correctly that one and the same theory should provide an explanation for national and international exchange.

Speaking of the classical theory, J. Viner accurately states his own conviction that '. . . it would be a mistake to carry its rehabilitation so far as to claim for it, even in its improved and modernized form, adequacy as a theory to guide policy in the present-day world'.[15] And he continues with the often quoted passage:

> The world has changed greatly, and is now a world of planned economies, of state trading, of substantially arbitrary and inflexible national price structures, and of managed instability in exchange rates. The classical theory is not directly relevant for such a world, and it may be that for such a world there is and can be no relevant *general* theory.[16]

The multiplicity of factors that may affect import and export prices, 'cannot be reduced to a *meaningful* simple formula',[17] and E.E. Hagen is right in claiming that '. . . there is no general basis for determining what a country's comparative advantage will be. One must simply look, to see what it is'.[18]

3. THE HECKSCHER-OHLIN THEORY

The basis now used is not one, but several factors of production. The production functions are assumed to be the same in every country: The same combination of factors of production yields the same production. The factor combination differs from product to product (e.g. production of textiles is more labour-intensive than that of cars). Hence, the various goods produced in a given country can be ranked according to their capital-intensiveness (or labour-intensiveness): this classification is assumed to be constant and is not influenced by alterations in the relative factor prices. (This is, of course, an unrealistic hypothesis.) In other words, factor-intensity reversal (so that textiles are produced more capital-intensively than cars) does not occur. But reasoning is not in real terms but in terms of money costs. The other hypotheses in the classical theory, however, have been adopted (such as constant returns and pure competition).

Under these conditions, differences in comparative costs are due to varying factor price ratios. The latter are determined by the quantity and quality of the manpower, capital goods and raw materials available in the various regions, and also by climatological conditions and the state of the soil. If labour (capital) is the relatively abundant and consequently cheap factor, a comparative advantage is obtained in the production and exportation of relatively labour-intensive (capital-intensive) goods.

Analysis on the basis of two or more factors is certainly more realistic, but the difficulties persist: These factors are not homogeneous.

Production techniques are not the same everywhere. Many goods can be produced, either capital-intensively or labour-intensively, at the same cost. As stated previously, the assumption that factor-intensity reversal cannot occur does not hold well in practice.

More than half the volume of international trade is between countries with roughly the same factor ratios. For this, the Heckscher-Ohlin theory can provide no explanation. Nor, since the factor endowments are assumed to be unchanged, can it account for substantial short-term changes in the pattern of trade. In the longer term, however, trade has an effect on factors: Instead of factor distribution accounting for the pattern of international trade, it is the latter that may give an idea of the former. (Trade, for instance, causes migration because of higher demand for labour in certain areas.)

Owing to government action (e.g. the fixing of minimum wages and social legislation), factor prices do not necessarily reflect the scarcity differences. For that matter, such scarcity differences are not always accorded the attention they deserve. For prestige reasons, preference is sometimes given to capital-intensive production where labour-intensive production is actually called for.

Although Ohlin's theory undoubtedly has an element of truth, it is clear from the foregoing that it is '... somewhat vague and conditional'.[19] G. Haberler too stresses that:

> ... with many factors of production, some of which are qualitatively incommensurable as between different countries, and with dissimilar production functions in different countries, no sweeping *a priori* generalizations concerning the composition of trade are possible.[20]

S. Mookerjee concludes a study devoted to the Heckscher-Ohlin theory in an identical way: 'In general . . . no definite *a priori* generalization concerning the composition of trade is possible'.[21]

4. EQUALISATION OF FACTOR PRICES

Ohlin also examined the repercussions of specialisation on prices of factors of production. International trade contributes to the evening-up of remunerations: the exchanging of endproducts is in some measure substituted for that of factors.[22]

Ohlin realises that complete equalisation is impossible, as the rise in prices of factors of production cannot but have its influence on the supply of such factors. Furthermore, demand for complementary factors will tend upwards, and thus an increase in the relevant prices is quite on the cards.

Endorsing a proposition already upheld by Heckscher in 1919, several authors – including F.D. Graham[23] in 1932, A.P. Lerner[24] in 1933 – have proved that, under certain conditions, complete equalisation will occur. The best-known contributions are those by P.A. Samuelson, who after the Second World War shows[25] that equalisation is in '. . . a wide variety of circumstances . . . inevitable'.[26] Complete geographical specialisation, which according to Samuelson in certain circumstances would be possible, does not necessarily bring about equality.[27] In this case too the hypotheses which he assumes for equalisation are unrealistic (similar wants, similar production functions, constant returns to scale, no transport costs or other impediments to trade, perfect competition: see §1). A few years later, he enlarges on this theme (the 'proof' is no longer confined to a two-region, two-commodity, two-factor case), but lays himself open to similar objections.[28] The transition from a simple to a complex model does not make analysis easier.[29] Later still he brings interest into his theorem.[30]

Apart from the contributions that square with Samuelson's point of view,[31] some articles pointing out its too absolute nature have appeared.[32] In this connection, it is often overlooked that Samuelson himself has drawn attention to its limitations.[33] Indeed, in a new model he concludes: 'After all, Bertil Ohlin's contention for partial but not total factor-price equalisation is essentialy vindicated in this technological model'.[34]

The conclusion to be drawn is that, as R. Harrod says, Samuelson's point of view has to be looked upon as a 'curiosum', not as a fundamental principle.[35] I.F. Pearce and S.F. James rightly point to the fact that generalisations on this subject are untenable: '... the effect of trade on factor prices depends on production functions, demand conditions and factor endowments, which must be investigated in each particular case if any prophecy is to be made'.[36] J. Bhagwati is not wide of the mark when he deplores in this respect '... that perhaps too great a proportion of the intellectual energy of trade theorists have been directed towards a question of limited utility'.[37]

5. THE EFFECTS OF ECONOMIC GROWTH ON FOREIGN TRADE

The long-term relation between national income and foreign trade prompted the following observation by Torrens as early as 1821: 'As the several nations of the world advance in wealth and populations, the commercial intercourse between them must gradually become less important and beneficial.' He assumed that trade between old and new countries would diminish because: '... as new countries advance in population, the cultivation of inferior soils must increase the cost of raising raw produce, and the division of labour reduces the expense of working it up ... the increasing value of raw produce must gradually check its exportation, and the falling value of wrought goods progressively prevent their importation'.[38]

In 1912 Werner Sombart (1863–1941) too gave it as his opinion that, after an initial expansion, the ratio between exports and national production would show a decrease.[39] Among the factors which, he says, account for this is the rising prosperity of the population together with the replacement of labour-intensive by capital-intensive production in other industries (textiles, leather).[40] Subsequently, he qualified his viewpoint by stating that exports would have an ever decreasing, or at least a *hardly increasing*,[41] share in total output.[42] F. Eulenburg in 1929 held the contrary opinion that foreign trade had become more important.[43] Subsequent appraisals were influenced by the great depression; thus as early as 1932 cyclical sensitiveness was considered to be the most important feature of world trade.[44]

On the basis of elaborate research which, on account of statistical limitations, relates only to developed countries, Kuznets recorded that, before the First World War trade proportions (by which is meant the ratio of exports and imports to the gross national product), based on quantities in terms of current prices, generally showed a rising trend.[45] In the case of Britain it climbed from 21.6 per cent in 1837–45 to 43.5 per cent in 1909–13. As regards the United States, there was a slight decline, namely from 12.9 in 1834–43 to 11.0 in 1904–13[46]. In the twenties, however, the ratios were generally a little lower than before the First World War. F. Hilgerdt, too, states that from 1871 until the thirties industrial growth '... far from rendering the countries concerned independent of foreign-produced articles, stimulated the importation of such articles, and ... imports tended to follow a course parallel to that of manufacturing activity'.[47] Only in the thirties did the ratio between production and trade change in a number of countries which stimulated domestic production to the detriment of imports.

According to Kuznets, after the Second World War trade proportions resumed a downward trend: in the late fifties they were, with one or two exceptions, significantly lower than in the period just before the First World War.[48] This evolution, however, did not persist. According to B. Nezeys, the ratio of world exports to gross world product increased continually during recent decades, rising from 10 per cent in 1970 to 18 per cent in 1980. Trade proportions for individual countries showed a similar trend. As compared with 1953, the proportion in 1982 was higher in almost all industrialized countries: 43 against 36 in the United Kingdom, 39 against 18 in France, 50 against 24 in the Federal Republic, 26 against 18 in Japan and 15 against 7 in the United States.[49]

Bearing in mind these and other contradictory[50] findings, the (in spite of everything) sparse data provided by Kuznets, and the subsequent trend of the relevant ratios in the sixties, we believe that the conclusions drawn by the same author a few years earlier, from long-term estimates for ten countries, are more in accordance with facts, namely that '... there is no prevalence of trends in one direction ...'.[51] This in his view was not '... surprising since the trend is affected by a wide variety of secularly changing factors whose different combinations produce different movements for different countries in different periods'.[52] Thus the importance of factors that are liable to have an adverse effect on international trade differs from country to country: the relative fall in demand for agricultural products, the relative increase in demand for services, the rapid dissemination of technological knowledge (through which the gains from innovations previously adopted are reduced), the ever-increasing use of capital goods (as a result of which the importance of the production factors nature and labour diminishes). Import substitution, considered by many less-developed countries a worth-while means of speeding up economic growth, has in the normal course an unfavourable influence. The importance of the factors promoting international trade (such as a decrease in transport costs; the appeal of foreign, though similar goods; innovations leading to exports of new products) also differs for each country.

6. TRADE AND ECONOMIC GROWTH

There are also contradictory views concerning the influence of foreign trade on growth. According to some of these views, an expansion of exports is a prerequisite for economic development[53]; according to others, it exercises an adverse influence. Whichever standpoint is adopted, the effect on economic policy is significant: in the one case, growth is to be secured by expanding exports; in the oher, by import substitution.

Those authors who regard trade as a favourable growth factor – notably Mill, Marshall, Viner, Haberler – point to the beneficial feedbacks, by which trade gives an impetus to growth: it widens the market, thus opening up the way for improved production processes (economies of large-scale production, improvements in technology) and curbs domestic monopolies. Many countries, moreover, are too small to pursue an intense industrialisation policy. Statistics seem to support this point of view. The ranking of industrial countries according to their annual growth rate of gross domestic product over the period 1960–82 reflects almost perfectly their ranking with respect to the growth rate of their export volumes.[54]

Especially since the Second World War, however, many authors have shown trade pessimism, at least in respect of less-developed countries. H.W. Singer[55] and G. Myrdal[56] hold extreme views on the subject. From the export-oriented enclaves in the less-developed countries, their argument runs, there are relatively few spill-overs (or spread effects) to the rest of the economy, so that dual societies are created or reinforced, while other industries and values may be destroyed (backwash effects). Trade does not contribute to the raising of the less-developed countries' living standards.

After pointing out that the economic growth of the 'new' states which sprang up in the past century – the United States, Canada, Argentina and Australia – was attributable to the substantial expansion of West-European, and especially British demand for foodstuffs and raw materials, Ragnar Nurkse[57] goes on to assert that the less-developed countries are no longer confronted with such an increasing demand (cf. the rise of synthetics) and that foreign trade, contrary to what happened in the last century, cannot be a prime mover of growth.

It has been stressed[58] that external demand is not necessarily the dominant factor in economic growth, which in the first place depends on internal structural or supply factors, and it is often these factors that account for the lag in exports suffered by the less-developed countries (for instance, population growth). Nor can it be argued that no effect has been exerted on the rest of the economy by these enclaves-[59] I.B. Kravis[60] shows that Nurkse's observations concerning exports do not hold good for the nineteenth and twentieth centuries; during the nineteenth century, both the United States and Australia showed few signs of export-led growth; countries with a low growth rate, such as India and Ceylon, achieved an export expansion similar to that of the United States and Canada. In the twentieth century, less-developed countries have even greater trade opportunities. If the proportion of exports accounted for by the less-developed countries as a group has declined, this can be explained by the fact that they:

> ... have not on the whole taken full advantage of world trade opportunities, often incorrectly attributing their difficulties to unfavourable external conditions when the most important problems have been at home.[61]

Exports can stimulate growth (as in the case of Britain from 1780 to 1800 and from 1850 to 1870). The rapid progress achieved by the Japanese economy is also usually attributed to export expansion.

In recent years the less-developed countries have attached more importance to their export potential. In UNCTAD (United Nations Conference on Trade and Development) publications, too, attention is drawn to the '... dominant role in stimulating ... overall economic growth ...'[62] of exports. Emphasis is placed on the fact that a better growth rate '... will depend on the expansion of demand in developed market economies and in the socialist countries at rates substantially above the average achieved in the last decade ...',[63] but little mention is made of the fact that in many cases domestic supply conditions should be improved. As long as '... sufficient social and political change, as well as economic change ...' has not been brought about '... to make the economy more responsive to the stimulus from trade ...',[64] there is little point in stimulating exports. Hence, according to H. Myint, it is '... paradoxical to describe export expansion policies as 'outward-looking' when their success vitally depends on domestic economic policies ...'.[65] During the period 1960–80, high growth rates of gross domestic product and export volumes persisted only in less-developed countries that have concentrated on exports of industrial commodities. In other less-developed countries they fell back in the early seventies after the overall expansion of world trade began to slow down.[66]

But if exporting can be a leading sector, it may also be a lagging sector.[67] The question whether or not export instability is damaging to growth also remains an open one.[68] There is now more or less of a consensus that no general pronouncements can be made on the relationship between trade and growth. Whether international trade is advantageous, neutral or injurious depends on a multiplicity of factors, including natural resource endowment, the kind of economic ownership (foreign or domestic) in the export sector, and the type of economic policy pursued. Whether an outward-looking or an inward-looking policy is preferable must not be determined by ideological considerations, but by the extent to which each policy, through the mobilisation of domestic production factors and the development of a different attitude, contributes to economic development. Moreover, the necessity of '. . . a case-by-case approach, tailoring policies to individual country situations . . .'[69] is being – as previously stressed – recognised more and more.

7. THE THEORY OF PURCHASING-POWER PARITY

The theory of purchasing-power parity, which was expounded in a modern formulation by Gustav Cassel after 1918,[70] states that the exchange rate or external value of a currency is determined by the domestic value or purchasing-power parity of the currencies concerned (in the case of fixed exchange rates, what proportion the purchasing power of price levels should bear to one another).

In the comparative version of the purchasing-power-parity theory, changes in purchasing power are analysed in relation to a specific reference period. However, it is difficult to find a reference period that is marked by a genuine equilibrium of exchange rates. We ought really to go back to pre-1914 days, but in the meantime every country's economic structure has changed.

The choice of indices is not easy.[71] Prices of many world-market products (e.g. commodities) show only slight differences on national markets, with the result that the corresponding index numbers prove to be of little use. More reliance is therefore to be placed on domestic-price indices (retail prices, wages, cost of living). If the cost-of-living index has risen more in one country than in another with a simultaneous wage increase, the adverse effects of these movements are experienced by costs and selling prices.

The price level is not always the decisive factor in the volume of imports and exports. A change in demand for certain commodities, such as that which may result from inventions (e.g. sodium nitrate and artificial fertilizer), may cause a disturbance of the balance-of-payments equilibrium without any alteration of the purchasing-power parity. Modifications of customs tariffs frequently have similar consequences.

The purchasing-power parity relates to only a part of the balance of payments. Capital movements are not taken into consideration (e.g. imports of securities). Cassel himself has pointed out that, apart from the purchasing-power parity, a great many other factors exercise an influence on exchange rates.

Many countries' currencies are indeed linked to that of another economically strong country. In such cases the exchange rate does not hinge on the purchasing-power parity, but the purchasing power of one currency is conditioned by that of another currency and the exchange rate between them.

But the purchasing-power-parity theory is the main determinant of the long-run equilibrium exchange rate. 'Over periods of time long enough for ratios of national price indexes to change radically, PPP (purchasing-power parity) may have considerable validity'.[72]

8. THE THEORY OF BALANCE-OF-PAYMENTS EQUILIBRIUM

The modern theory relates restoration of equilibrium more closely to the fluctuations in employment and the national income than was the case of the gold standard system. This theory applies only when there is no full employment (constant prices). It is based on the assumptions that the marginal propensities to save and to import remain constant and that it is always possible to finance deficits, which in point of fact is not so. It further postulates that exports result from current production (and not from stocks). In the less-developed countries, import requirements are becoming so heavy (demonstration effect) that the theory cannot be applied to these areas.

Like the classical doctrine, this theory is based on an automatically operating mechanism, but the balance of payments is not necessarily brought into equilibrium in the modern theory. Instead of price fluctuations, it is mainly variations in the level of employment and the national income that perform a regulatory function. In fact, both income and price fluctuations play a role, but their importance varies from country to country.

Yet every country at least tries to maintain stability in the national income, employment and prices and therefore endeavours to counter-act such oscillations. It does not acquiesce in an equilibrium rate of exchange that has large-scale unemployment as its concomitant. Such a policy contributes to the uncertainty surrounding an automatic correction of the balance of payments.

9. CONCLUSION

From the foregoing it is obvious that neither the theory of comparative cost nor the Heckscher-Ohlin theory can really be called satisfactory. H.W.J. Wijnholds justifiably believes that 'too much time has been wasted already in patching up a theory (of comparative cost) that is faulty in its very foundations'.[73] To conceal its draw-backs, the theory of comparative cost is sometimes formulated so vaguely (for instance, the 'law' of comparative prices) that it is certainly not capable of explaining the true situation.

The fact is that an explanation is sought for differences in prices, as the decisions made by importers and exporters are based on them. The theory of comparative cost assumes that prices in international exchange are a reflection of comparative costs. This implies, in particular, that the price system operates in a highly flexible manner (pure competition), that exchange rates are selected appropriately and that there are no barriers to trade (which, as already pointed out, are unrealistic hypotheses). In many cases, international division of labour can only be accounted for by historical or political circumstances. International restrictive agreements frequently influence international trade. The Heckscher-Ohlin theory is somewhat applicable to natural resources, but the influence of this factor is steadily declining as a result of the downward trend of transport costs.

There is no simple explanation for international trade because of the multiplicity of factors that may affect import and export prices (e.g. the importance of the domestic market and the technological lead).

Since it 'is impossible from theoretical or analytical considerations alone to determine in detail in what products or branches the 'comparative advantages' of a given economy are most likely to lie in the future'[74] the notion of 'revealed comparative advantage' has been introduced.[75] But it is as unsatisfactory as the 'revealed preferences'.[76] No more can a single theory explain the behaviour of exchange rates. Yet, despite the foregoing objections and its limited applicability, the theory of purchasing-power parity may, in some circumstances, yield concrete data.[77] In this respect, the theory of balance-of-payments equilibrium is disappointing.

NOTES

1 G. Haberler, *The theory of international trade* (London: William Hodge, 1936), pp. 175 et seq.

2 J.S. Mill, *Principles of political economy,* 2nd ed. vol. III (London: Longmans, Green, Roader and Dyer, 1869), Chap. 18.

3 J.A. L'Huillier, *Théorie et pratique de la coopération économique internationale* (Paris: M.Th. Génin, 1957), p. 555.

4 R.W. Stevens, New ideas in the theory of international trade, *The American Economic Review,* June 1951, p. 387.

5 J.C. Perrin, *Les graphiques théoriques des analyses du commerce international* (Paris: Institut de Science Economique Appliquée, 1956), p. 34.

6 J. Wemelsfelder, De techniek der collectieve indifferentiecurven en het optimale invoerrecht', *De Economist,* Jan. 1953, p. 53. G. Haberler also stated that the collective indifference curve was '. . . still far from a satisfactory solution', *A survey of international trade theory,* op. cit., p. 16.

7 Cf. also O. D'Alauro, Le curve di indifferenza 'per una communitá': analisi critica, *Economia Internazionale,* Feb. 1954.

8 M.A.G. van Meerhaeghe, *International economics* (London: Longman, 1972).

9 C.P. Kindleberger and P.H. Lindert, *International economics,* 4th ed. (Homewood Ill.: R. Irwin, 1982), p. 42.

10 J.S. Mill, op. cit., Vol. III, Ch. 18, p. 353.

11 F. Edgeworth, The pure theory of international trade, in *Papers relating to political economy* (London: Macmillan, 1925), pp. 31–43.

12 A. Marshall, *The pure theory of foreign trade. The pure theory of domestic values.* No. 1 in Series of reprints of scarce tracts in economic and political science (London: The London School of Economics and Political Science, 1930).

13 J. Viner, *International economics* (Glencoe Ill.: The Free Press, 1951), p. 547.

14 F.D. Graham, *The theory of international values* (Princeton: Princeton University Press, 1948).

15 J. Viner, op. cit., p. 16.

16 J. Viner, op. cit., p. 16; J. Viner explains his point of view in International trade theory and its present-day relevance, in *Foreign agricultural trade. Selected readings,* ed. R.L. Tontz (Ames: The Free Press, 1966); see also J.H. Williams, International trade theory and policy – some current issues, *The American Economic Review,* May 1951, p. 420: 'International trade is so complex, so subject to heterogeneous conditions and to ceaseless changes in conditions, that it seems to me almost . . . naive to speak of *the* theory of international trade . . .'.

17 H. Bockelmann, *Zur Kritik der klassischen Tradition in der Aussenhandelstheorie* (Frankfurt/Main: Fritz Knapp, 1958), p. 47.

18 E.E. Hagen, op. cit., p. 445. See in this connection the 'revealed' comparative advantages of B. Balassa, *Trade liberalization among industrial countries: objectives and alternatives* (New York: McGraw-Hill, 1967), p. 86 et seq.

19 M. Diab, *The United States capital position and the structure of its foreign trade* (Amsterdam: North Holland, 1956), p. 11.

20 G. Haberler, *A survey of international trade theory* (Princeton: Princeton University Press, 1955), p. 25.

21 S. Mookerjee, *Factor endowments and international trade. A statement and appraisal of the Heckscher-Ohlin theory* (Bombay: Asia Publishing House, 1958), p. 95.

22 B. Ohlin, *Interregional and international trade* (rev. ed.), op. cit., pp. 24–29.

23 F.D. Graham, The theory of international values, *The Quarterly Journal of Economics*, Aug. 1932.

24 A.P. Lerner, Factor prices and international trade, *Economica*, February 1952 (unpublished lecture at the London School of Economics in December 1933).

25 P.A. Samuelson, International trade and the equalisation of factor prices, *The Economic Journal*, June 1948; *id.*, International factor price equalisation again, *The Economic Journal*, June 1949. See minor corrections to this text in J.E. Meade, The equalisation of factor prices: the two-country, two-factor, three-product case, *Metroeconomica*, Dec. 1950, p. 133, footnote; P.A. Samuelson, A comment on factor price equalisation, *Review of Economics and Statistics*, no. 49, 1951–52, p. 221, footnote.

26 P.A. Samuelson, International trade and the equalisation of factor prices, art. cit., p. 169.

27 Ibid., p. 178.

28 P.A. Samuelson, Prices of factors and goods in general equilibrium, *Review of Economics and Statistics*, no. 54, 1953–54.

29 H.G. Johnson, Factor endowments, international trade and factor prices, *The Manchester School of Economic and Social Studies*, Sept. 1957, reproduced in the work by the same author: *International trade and economic growth* (London: G. Allen & Unwin, 1958), Ch. 1.

30 P.A. Samuelson, Equalisation by trade of the interest rate along with the real wage, in *Trade, growth and the balance of payments. Essays in honor of Gottfried Haberler*, eds. R.E. Caves, H.G. Johnson and P.B. Kenen (Chicago: Rand McNally, 1965).

31 See M.O. Clement, R.L. Pfister and K.J. Rothwell, *Theoretical issues in international economics* (Boston: Houghton Mifflin, 1968), Ch. 1, for a bibliographical survey.

32 See, e.g., O. D'Alauro, I prezzi dei fattori produttivi e la teoria dello scambio internazionale, *Economia Internazionale*, Feb. 1959; A. Land, Factor endowments and factor prices, *Economica*, May 1959.

33 P.A. Samuelson, International factor price equalisation again, art. cit., pp. 195–97.

34 P.A. Samuelson, Ohlin was right, *The Swedish Journal of Economics*, Dec. 1971.

35 R. Harrod, Factor-price relations and free trade, *The Economic Journal*, June 1958, p. 255.

36 I.F. Pearce and S.F. James, The factor-price equalisation myth, *Review of Economics and Statistics*, no. 49, 1951–52, p. 119; see also T. Balogh, Factor intensities of American foreign trade and technical progress, *Review of Economic Studies*, Aug. 1963, p. 427.

37 J. Bhagwati, The pure theory of international trade: a survey, *The Economic Journal*, March 1964, p. 32.

38 R. Torrens, *An essay on the production of wealth* (1821). *With an introductory essay 'Robert Torrens and American economic thought' by Joseph Dorfman* (Reprints of economic classics, New York: A. Kelley, 1965), p. 288.

39 W. Sombart, *Die Deutsche Volkswirtschaft im neunzehnten Jahrhundert und im Anfang*

des 20. Jahrhunderts. Eine Einführung in die Nationalökonomie, 7th ed. (Berlin: G. Bondi, 1927), pp. 369–70; the 1st ed. was published in 1912.

40 W. Sombart, op. cit., p. 370.

41 Our italics.

42 Ibid., p. 373.

43 F. Eulenburg, *Aussenhandel und Aussenhandelspolitik. Die internationalen Wirtschaftsbeziehungen* (Tübingen: J.C.B. Möhr-Siebeck, 1929), p. 70.

44 M. Victor, Das sogenannte Gesetz der abnehmenden Aussenhandelsbedeutung, *Weltwirtschaftliches Archiv,* Band 36, Heft 1, 1932, p. 82.

45 S. Kuznets, *Modern economic growth. Rate, structure and spread* (New Haven: Yale University Press, 1966).

46 Ibid., pp. 312–13.

47 F. Hilgerdt, *Industrialisation and foreign trade* (Geneva: League of Nations, 1945), p. 118.

48 S. Kuznets, op. cit., p. 318.

49 B. Nezeys, *Commerce international, croissance et développement* (Paris: Economica, 1985), pp. 55–57.

50 See, for instance, K. Deutsch, C. Bliss and A. Eckstein, Population, sovereignty, and the share of foreign trade, *Economic Development and Cultural Change,* July 1962.

51 S. Kuznets, *Six lectures on economic growth* (Glencoe Ill.: Free Press, 1959), p. 100.

52 Ibid., p. 103.

53 Cf. B. Balassa, Export incentives and export performance in developing countries. A comparative analysis, *Weltwirtschaftliches Archiv,* 1978, Heft 1; A.O. Krueger, Trade policy as an input to development, *The American Economic Review,* May 1980.

54 B. Nezeys, op. cit., pp. 46–50.

55 H.W. Singer, U.S. foreign investment in underdeveloped areas. The distribution of gains between investing and borrowing countries, *The American Economic Review,* May 1950, p. 478.

56 G. Myrdal, *An international economy. Problems and prospects* (New York: Harper and Brothers, 1956), p. 231; id., *Rich lands and poor* (New York: Harper and Brothers, 1957).

57 *Equilibrium and growth in the world economy. Economic essays by Ragnar Nurkse,* ed. G. Haberler and R.M. Stern (Cambridge, Mass.: Harvard University Press, 1961), pp. 242 et seq.

58 See, e.g., G. Haberler, *International trade and development* (Cairo: National Bank of Egypt, 1959); A.K. Cairncross, Patterns of trade and development, *Kyklos,* Fasc. 4, 1960; id., International trade and economic development, *Economica,* Aug. 1961.

59 R. Vernon, Foreign-owned enterprises in the developing countries, in *Public policy,* ed. D. Montgomery and A. Smithies (Cambridge, Mass.: Harvard University Press, 1966).

60 I.B. Kravis, Trade as a handmaiden of growth: similarities between the nineteenth and twentieth centuries, *The Economic Journal,* Dec. 1970.

61 Ibid., p. 870.

62 United Nations Conference on Trade and Development, *Review of international trade and development 1970, Part I. Recent trends in trade and development. Report by the secretariat of UNCTAD* (Geneva, Aug. 26, 1970), p. 70.

63 Ibid., p. 72.

64 G.M. Meier, *International trade and development* (New York: Harper and Row, 1964), p. 191.

65 H. Myint, Dualism and the internal integration of the underdeveloped countries, *Banca Nazionale del Lavoro Quarterly Review,* June 1970, p. 154. He considers the use of the term

'inward-looking' policies equally paradoxical '. . . when their main underlying emphasis is on economic aid (and trade concessions) to be administered from outside', ibid., p. 153).

66 B. Nezeys, op. cit., p. 51.

67 T.K. Morrison, *Manufactured exports from developing countries* (New York: Praeger, 1976), p. 4.

68 L. Stein, Export instability and development. A review of some recent findings, *Banca Nazionale del Lavoro Quarterly Review,* Sept, 1977, p. 289.

69 M.G. de Vries, Trade and exchange policy and economic development, *Oxford Economic Papers,* March 1966, p. 39.

70 G. Cassel, The present situation of the foreign exchanges, *The Economic Journal,* March 1966; id., Abnormal deviations in international exchanges, *The Economic Journal,* Sept. 1918; id., *Money and foreign exchange after 1914* (New York: Macmillan, 1923).

71 J.A. Frenkel, Purchasing-power parity. Doctrinal perspective and evidence from the 1920s, *Journal of International Economics,* May 1978.

72 P. Isard, *Exchange-rate determination. A survey of popular views and recent models* (Princeton N.J.: Princeton University, May 1978), p. 8.

73 H.W.J. Wijnholds, *International trade and payments. An introduction to the theory of international trade, commercial policy and other economic relations* (Pretoria: The Academic Press, s.d.: 1955), p. 14.

74 Some aspects of manufacturing development in southern Europe: production, trade and transfer of technology, *Economic Bulletin for Europe,* 1972, no. 2, p. 75.

75 B. Balassa, Trade liberalisation of 'revealed' comparative advantages, *Manchester School of Economic and Social Studies* 1965.

76 A.L. Hillman, Observations on the relation between 'revealed comparative advantages' and comparative advantages as indicated by pre-trade relative prices, *Weltwirtschaftliches Archiv,* Heft 2, 1980.

77 See, e.g., N. Thygesen, Inflation and exchange rates. Evidence and policy guidelines for the European Community, *Journal of International Economics,* May 1978.

9. ECONOMIC DOCTRINES AND ECONOMIC POLICY

Before examining in the next chapter how economic theory influences economic policy, it is worthwhile to dwell upon this relationship in the past. What were the repercussions of economic doctrines upon the policies of their times?

Economic doctrines, or economic ideas, must not be confused with economic history, which relates to economic facts – in other words, history studied from the standpoint of economics. Although communication and knowledge of facts is sometimes indispensable for ideas to be understood – they interact upon each other – it is best not to mingle the two concepts. The history of economic ideas cannot easily be divorced from the history of ideas in general.

The Greeks, who were first and foremost politicians, never thought in purely economic terms. Nor did the Romans devote much attention to economic problems.

Although labour became more respectable during the Middle Ages and was no longer done by slaves, the Church condemned any unrestrained craving for wealth. The development of trade prompted the clergy, the intellectuals of the time, to deliver judgments on economic questions. In these they invariably adopted an ethical standpoint. Thomas Aquinas (1226–74) defined the position of the Church towards the economic problems of the day: Interest was prohibited (time was God's and not marketable), whereas a compensation for the use of land was permissible. This was not regarded as exploitation but as a return for the natural properties of the soil made available (the Church was a major landholder). Later on, a moderate interest was allowed to be charged in respect of loans for non-consumption purposes which involved the lender in disadvantages (*damnum emergens*) or elimination of benefits (*lucrum cessans*). The price could only be a reward for the labour (*justum pretium*).

This distrustful attitude towards (high) interest secured a place in society for the Jews (who were excluded from crafts and trades): '. . . as money-lenders they performed a role essential to the kings' continued need of money'.[1]

1. MERCANTILISM

The setting-up of nation states and the discovery of America (1492) had profound economic repercussions. The rationalist spirit gained more and more ground; profit-seeking assumed unusually large proportions. The formation of national armies made vast monetary demands on the sovereign rulers. The influence of the state increased at the expense of the authority of the Church.

The entire body of measures designed to make the state as powerful and as rich as possible was called the mercantilist system. The principal means employed to fulfil this aim were acquisition of a maximum amount of precious metals and the pursuance of an active population policy. Mercantilism embodied the precept that states possessing gold and silver (e.g. Spain) should endeavour to keep such metals, exports being prohibited. Other countries exerted every effort to obtain gold and silver; if they had no mines to develop, they had to stimulate imports of precious metals. This could only be done if there was a favourable trade balance.

The mercantilists had a one-sided view of wealth. The importance of money was overestimated. Even so, an increase in the quantity of money was necessary at time in order to counteract barter, which was induced by the lack of currency. Hence, selfcentred trade policies developed, often producing adverse consequences. The bullionist policy upheld by Spain was especially pernicious.

Numerous objections were subsequently raised to mercantilism. In the circumstances then prevailing, a great many measures were characterized by a high degree of realism. The anxiety concerning the demographic trend, for instance, was understandable after long-drawn-out wars had caused the population to drop considerably.

2. PHYSIOCRACY

The physiocrats reacted against Colbertism, the industrial form of mercantilism, and were therefore opposed to state intervention and to neglect of agriculture. Their underlying principle was that only agriculture should be considered productive. But by the same reasoning taxes had to be charged solely on agriculture.

The physiocrats were the first economic school. Proceeding from specific principles, they developed a coherent theory; in addition, they brought the 'natural laws' concept to the forefront.

In order to stimulate agriculture, prices of agrarian products must be freely determined and, for example, any ban on exports is frowned upon. Absolute freedom is the best way to achieve prosperity. Everyone must be able to seek his own interests without hindrance from the government; the individual's interests are at one with society's. Nevertheless, the state must be strong enough to safeguard freedom of action ('legal despotism' theory). If the natural laws cannot exercise their influence free from restrictions, society must be changed in the desired manner (the natural order or the order willed by God).

The solicitude for agriculture followed the fashion of the time. The physiocrats had no influence on economic policy (if we exclude small experiments in Baden and in Tuscany). Their success was 'primarily a succès de salon'.[2]

3. THE CLASSICAL SCHOOL

The 'classical' authors claimed that industry is as much a productive branch of activity as agriculture. They considered labour to be the basis of value. But they adopted the concept of natural order and developed it further. Self-interest, the basis of human action, generates maximum performance (beneficial egoism).

Adam Smith's (1723–90) optimism was not shared by Thomas Malthus (1766–1834), according to whom pauperism is an inevitable phenomenon, caused by overpopulation. If positive checks (such as wars) do not work, preventive checks (moral restraint) must be applied. This theory had some influence on the public assistance policy of the day.

The assumptions of the classical authors reproduce 'tolerably well the actualities of the time ... Practically all economists *believed* ... that ... laissez-faire was the general rule for the administration of a nation's economic affairs ...'. They realized 'the superiority ... of the businessmen's administration of the productive resources over what could possibly have been expected from the public official of his day'.[3]

Since the publication of Smith's *Wealth of Nations* (1776) the ideas of liberty progressed everywhere. But in the last third of the 19th century criticism was forthcoming from various quarters. It occurs at the same time as or follows political changes. In the United Kingdom, for example, important shifts in electoral power in 1867 and in 1884 (sometimes supported by classical authors, such as John Stuart Mill and William Stanley Jevons) brought about changes in economic policy's objectives. Adroit politicians advocated progressive taxation and equally dextrous economists found arguments in favour of such taxes (although no economic proof of the superiority of progressive taxes can be adduced).

Opposition to the classical school found expression in 1841 (List's *Das Nationale System der politischen Oekonomie*), 1867 (the first volume of *Das Kapital*), 1872 (creation of the *Verein für Sozialpolitik*) and in political catholicism. The classical edifice was endowed with a more modern aspect in 1871 (Menger's *Grundsätze*).

The adherents of the protectionist movement denied that the benefits of international trade are experienced by all nations. According to Friedrich List (1798–1846), a forerunner of the historical school, the economic development process went through the following stages: (a) nomadism and (b) sedentariness, the latter being subdivided into the following phases: (i) agriculture; (ii) agriculture and manufacturing (iii) agriculture, manufacturing and trade. The transition from phase (ii) to (iii) occurs when manufacturing (or agriculture) has developed sufficiently to produce at lower costs than those ruling in other countries. As long as this has not been achieved, protectionism is legitimate in order to promote the development of domestic agriculture and manufacturing. In List's view, the United Kingdom and France had already passed this phase, but Germany had not. List's infant-industry theory is not *in se* opposed to free trade.

In point of fact, these phases are interwoven; trade sometimes exists before manufacturing. Different classifications were drawn up, mostly based on secondary factors.

The historical school contests the universality of economic laws, which are limited by time and space, and endeavours to establish development laws (*Wirtschaftsstufen*). Several of the young historical school's adherents advocated social reforms (including progressive income taxes, old age pensions and sickness insurance). In 1872 they founded the *Verein für Sozialpolitik* at Eisenach, which had a considerable influence on social and political developments in Germany (especially the social legislation introduced by Bismarck).

According to Jean Charles de Sismondi (1773–1842), mechanization is the scourge of the working class. His criticism of the capitalist system made him a forerunner of socialism; his call for a return to a corporative society brought him closer to the romantic movement, which does not accept human egoism as a basis for economic science. The most prominent representatives of this movement were German Catholic authors (notably Adam Heinrich Müller, 1779–1829). The Church favoured social reforms and a corporative organisation (cf. *Rerum Novarum,* 1891 and *Quadragesimo Anno,* 1931).

While anti-liberal tendencies were reinforced, the free trade movement remained strong and could prevent protectionist measures. Most economists, even those like Alfred Marshall who were in favour of progressive taxation, defended free trade. But free trade's success was not due to a doctrinal victory. Nor is the repeal in 1846 of the Corn Laws of 1815 to be accounted for by that factor.[4] This was mainly the response 'to shift of political and economic power'.[5]

4. SOCIALISM

In contrast with the liberals, socialists do not believe that individual efforts to secure a higher income bring prosperity to the entire population. What is needed is cooperation, which can only be achieved through fundamental equality of rights and opportunities. Marx's work is 'an unsuccessful attempt to prove scientifically the inevitable collapse of capitalism in Western Europe'.[6] Marx anticipates important aspects of the development of capitalism (e.g. economic concentration) but is mistaken concerning other fields (e.g. the *Verelendungstheorie*). His explanation of these phenomena is, however, based on a faulty premise (the classical theory of value).

Why history is to be considered as class struggle, why a classless society will come into being (and why people will be happier in such a society), is not explained. In this respect, Marxism can be compared with a religion. Non-believers are mere 'bourgeois'. There are classes (for which there is no specific definition, even from Marx) within the 'working class' in the Soviet Union, as in the United States. However, in the Soviet Union, the ruling class does not own but control the factors of production. The one elite succeeds the other. Elimination of private property does not in itself create a paradise on earth. This is evident in the Soviet Union, where a dictatorial 'transition period' has already been in progress for 70 years and where

> after all the attempts at socialist emulation, the leaders . . . have admitted that 'in quiet periods' the mass of workers does not act as militants should, that this elite itself, after the victory, has gradually wearied of practising

> the virtue of asceticism, and that inequality of remuneration has, in a modern economy, remained both indispensable and inevitable. Proletarians are human beings, not angels. The revolutionaries, who start by considering them as angels, end by treating them like animals.[7]

Neither Marx's work nor that of his followers contains a great deal about the future organization of the socialist society. The economic theory of socialism was mainly formulated by nonsocialists at a later stage,

In the Western European countries, rapid economic progress induces most socialist leaders to adopt reformism. Eduard Bernstein (1850–1932), in *Die Voraussetzungen des Sozialismus und die Aufgaben der Sozialdemokratie* (Stuttgart 1899, 3rd ed., 1921; English ed. *Evolutionary Socialism: A Critique and Affirmation,* London 1909), criticizes several of Marx's principal standpoints and urges development of the socialist movement by means of cooperatives, workers' associations and participation in parliamentary activity (e.g. for the purposes of social legislation).

Between the two world wars, attention has been devoted, partly as a result of the socialist parties' being concerned in the government of some western countries (due to the extension of voting rights), to the operation of a planned economy, the nationalisation of the key industries and the application of social-security systems. The planned economy was championed as early as the thirties by a Belgian, Hendrik de Man (1885-1953), who, however, became better known for his psychological and sociological theory of socialism (*Zur Psychologie des Sozialismus,* 1926; *Vermassung und Kulturverfall,* 1951).

Since the Second World War, reformists have pointed out that revolutions by proletarians lead to dictatorship and to oppression. It is not so much the distribution of property between various groupings but rather the distribution of power that is important. (In other words, the aim must not be nationalisation but economic democracy.)

And C. Bruclain (pseudonym for a collective authorship) states that '... the problem of ownership is now ... of secondary importance. A dynamic private enterprise can in certain respects be more 'socialist' than an inefficient public enterprise'.

The efficiency of the Western economic system has to be accorded due weight.

If it is to avoid becoming inefficient or deviating towards tyranny, *modern*

> *socialism* must safeguard human liberties and come to terms with the fact that the masses are not likely to sacrifice the various forms of individual satisfaction which capitalism offers or promises them particularly in *Western Europe.*[8]

Most Neo-Marxist authors observe with regret that the workers' standard of living has risen considerably under capitalism and that they accept the contemporary economic order. They try to make the workers realize that they are suffering from alienation ('alienation' being a word that is used in widely differing senses; e.g. to point out that labour does not bring satisfaction but only fatigue, that people become estranged, today the concept is used in a vague and very broad sens: the harmful repercussions of capitalism on human life). It is noteworthy that Neo-Marxist literature is filled with egalitarian phraseology, yet it also indicates the necessity of a new elite that will decide upon what is good for the masses. It is striking that Neo-Marxist theories are 'qualitatively on a much lower level than Marx's theories'.[9] Even champions of the former consider the economic analysis in Neo-Marxist publications '. . . a little weak'.[10] In most cases, a critical approach is lacking. The capitalist system is responsible for all real and imaginary evils. Thus, the greater prosperity of the West is attributed to colonial exploitation. (There is no attempt to explain what the basis is of Sweden's and Switzerland's standard of living, or why Portugal is not so rich as these two countries). Hence, G.Th.J. Delfgaauw[11] rightly says:

> . . . the attraction exerted by Marxism on some intellectuals in these days is due not to the analytical significance of the system but to revolutionary pathos or to the promise to create a new paradise on earth after the revolution . . .[11]

5. CONCLUSION

Economic doctrines have no significant impact on economic policy. Some authors believe that they did during the mercantilist period.[12] But mercantilism is a series of measures designed to make the state more powerful rather than a doctrine. No effect at all originates from physiocracy. While it is not claimed that the classical theory had no repercussions on policy, the conduct of the state is influenced more by changing political and social factors. The position of the Church is often more important than economic doctrine.

Since socialist theory – which has more of a bearing on social history – does not furnish any directive concerning economic policy, it is impossible to study the relation between theory and policy in the USSR. The reformist programmes in other countries – which some socialist parties were able to carry out wholly or partially – are influenced by social and political factors, not by economic theories.

NOTES

1 B.W. Tuchman, *A distant mirror. The calamitous 14th century* (Middlesex: Penguin, 1979), p. 110.

2 J.S. Schumpeter, *History of economic analysis,* ed. E.B. Schumpeter (London: Allen and Unwin, 1984), p. 230.

3 Ibid., p. 249.

4 See, however, P. Mendès-France and G. Adam, Economics and action: introduction, in *Economic policy. Readings in political economy,* ed. W.D. Grampp and E.T. Weiler (Homewood Ill: R. Irwin, 1956), p. 4; C. Watrin, Ökonomische Theorie und Wirtschaftliches Handeln in *Theorie und Realität. Ausgewählte Aufsätze zur Wissenschaftslehre der Sozialwissenschaften,* 2e ed. (Tübingen: J.C.B. Möhr (Paul Siebeck), 1972), p. 363.

5 G. Stigler, *The economist as preacher* (Oxford: Basil Blackwell, 1982), p. 65.

6 A. van Doorn, *Uitleiding uit de Marxistische economie* (Leiden: H.E. Stenfert Kroese, 1978), p. 3.

7 R. Aron, *Les désillusions du progrès* (Paris: Calmann-Lévy, 1969), p. 134.

8 C. Bruclain, *Le socialisme et l'Europe* (Paris: Editions du Seuil, 1965), p. 50 and p. 57.

9 L. Hoffman, Wetenschap of religie?, *Economisch-Statistische Berichten,* 26 april 1972, p. 401. Cf. M. Olson in a book review: 'There is no way that the vast impact of Marx' work can be explained in terms of any intellectual discoveries or long line of cumulative research that it has generated among his followers' (*Journal of Economic Literature,* June 1985, p. 624).

10 B. Ward, op. cit., p. 79.

11 G.Th.J. Delfgaauw, De economie van Herbert Marcuse en zijn geestesverwanten, in *Schaarste en Welvaart.* Opstellen aangeboden aan Prof. Dr. P. Hennipman ter gelegenheid van zijn vijfentwintigjarig hoogleraarschap aan de universiteit van Amsterdam (Leiden: Stenfert Kroese, 1971), p. 35.

12 P. Mendès-France, art. cit., p. 3; C. Watrin, art. cit., p. 352.

10. ECONOMIC THEORY AND ECONOMIC POLICY

After a digression upon welfare theory, a branch of economics concerned with efficiency, the most important contemporary economic theories and their impact upon economic policy are dealt with. Finally, we describe the main causes of disagreement among economists.

I. WELFARE THEORY

Welfare theory sets out to study value judgments and facts in combination. The practitioners of welfare theory, who do not necessarily accept that it is part of the economist's task to state the aims of economic policy, nevertheless maintain that economics must decide which economic system will yield maximum utility or maximum welfare.

A. Smith maintained that this would result from the free exchange of production factors; by seeking profits each individual helps to maximize the common good (by the working of the 'invisible hand').[1] Later on, V. Pareto proved this mathematically,[2] but proceeding from rather unrealistic hypotheses(e.g. perfect competition, a stationary economy and a given income distribution, no social wants).[3] Under perfect competition, there is no point in changing the distribution of goods: prices of goods are proportional to their marginal utility, factor prices to their marginal productivity. A change in income would lessen the satisfaction of at least one consumer or the output of at least one producer.

Numerous authors have elaborated on welfare theory, but since they have further amplified its unreality, little use can be derived from their directives. Thus the Pareto theorem is only valid for a given income distribution. Since one cannot prove that any given distribution is better than any other, welfare theory assumes that government will establish a scale of social preferences, which is supposed to aggregate the preferences of the whole community. But this assumption disregards social wants, and also the view that some wants should be discouraged and others encouraged.[4] Welfare theory is of little practical value. Even if, for instance, we knew all those who would benefit or be harmed by a certain measure (which we do not), it would still be impossible to compare subjective judgments of the burdens and benefits concerned (interpersonal utility comparisons being impossible). Hence, F.A. Lutz's remark: 'It is . . . no miracle that only a handful of English theorists concern themselves with this side of welfare economics.[5]

Welfare theory is the basis of cost-benefit analysis. The advantage of cost-benefit analysis consists in making a (complete) list of the pro's and con's of a given policy measure.[6] But precise conclusions are impossible (interpersonal utility comparisons being ruled out) and in governments' investment decisions they are of little use.[7]

2. KEYNESIANISM

The General Theory of J.M. Keynes (1883–1946)[8] brought about an important change in economic theory in several areas. Although no model of clarity – P.A. Samuelson calls it 'a badly written book, poorly organized; . . . arrogant, bad-tempered, polemical, and not overly-generous in its acknowledgements' – it immediately had a marked influence. Samuelson, indeed, concludes the passage in question with the words: 'in short, it is the work of a genius'.[9]

Keynes does not accept the long-term reasoning of the classical authors ('in the long run we are all dead'). He stresses the danger of stagnation in the capitalist countries. He sees two ways of obviating such a situation – increasing consumption by better income distribution, and expanding public works.

As a result of the discussion provoked by the *General Theory,* more importance is now attached to macroeconomics and economic statistics.

Keynes also had his influence on political thought. Although not a socialist himself, he exercised a considerable influence on the socialist philosophy. For some of his followers Keynesian economics was 'only a tool for furthering left-wing politics at the level of intellectual debate'.[10]

According to Keynesian theory, the quantity of money has little effect on prices. Hence the opposition of its adherents to the monetarists. They too favour income policies.

During the fifties and the sixties Keynesianism was prevalent among economists. Many Keynesians now take account of the postwar experience and supplement the theory with treatment of the supply side.[11]

The Keynesian policy may be useful in a period of crisis or depression. It becomes dangerous and gives rise to inflation when applied indiscriminately.

3. MONETARISM

In the inflationary seventies monetarism replaces keynesianism as the dominant theory. It adopts a quantity-theory approach and supports monetary 'rules' (in terms of a monetary aggregate).

M. Friedman first advocated an automatic annual increase of 4 to 5 per cent (later 2 per cent) in the money supply, in view of his reservations *vis-à-vis* governments which allow the money supply to grow out of all proportion and thus accelerate inflation. He does, however, admit that approximately 50 per cent of variations in economic activity cannot be explained by the money supply. Budgetary policy remains important, assuming that governments, in pursuing this policy, do so in complete impartiality and base it on economic considerations. The same applies to monetary policy. Accordingly, central banks must not be subservient to governments, and must be in a position of total independence in taking the necessary decisions.[12]

The Bank for International Settlements stresses the value of monetary targets:

> It might well be helpful if more countries were to commit themselves publicly to a target for the growth of one or several of their monetary aggregates. Such an announcement could be useful on two counts. First, it might impose a constraint on government policy – especially on the monetary financing of the public sector. Secondly, it might also have a dampening effect on inflationary expectations by conveying to the public, as well as to labour and management, that the authorities were committing themselves fully to the objective of mastering inflation.[13]

Monetary policy must be applied with caution: the velocity of money is not constant and there is much discussion concerning the money concept to be used. Results of Friedman studies[14] are called in question.[15] In contradistinction to Keynesianism, monetarism is opposed to an activist economic policy.

Related to monetarism are the public-choice, supply-side and rational-expectations theories.

The public-choice economists apply the methods of economic analysis (and its individualistic postulates) to the state. The politician, the bureaucrat, the voter pursue their personal interest, not the public interest.

Supply-side economists are interested in the supply side of economic activity, as a reaction to economists interested mainly in demand. They are not original, since the writings of classical authors contain similar points of view, but they have the merit of insisting – at the right moment – on the necessity of investment-increasing measures (tax reduction and deregulation).

Rational expectations are based on knowledge of the market. They take account of economic policy measures in operation or announced. The rational-expectations economists believe that markets are working efficiently and they are also opposed to government intervention.

4. EFFECTS ON ECONOMIC POLICY

Numerous versions exist of Keynesianism and monetarism and it makes the battle between the proponents of these versions opaque and confused. Nevertheless, there is a tendency to rapprochement between the two main theories.

After the Second World War the prescriptions of Keynesian policy (especially an increase of government spending) did not yield the expected results. They even caused a worsening of the economic situation in many countries. By expanding demand indiscriminately this policy led to more inflation, instead of more output.

But economists are not to be blamed: *politicians* pursue economic policy and they apply the easy directives of Keynesian policy at the wrong moment and with wrong degrees of intensity.

In many cases, governments have spent more than they have earned, not for economic, but for political reasons. This is quite normal, since they have an eye only to the next election. In the United States the public works programme 'launched in 1963 to speed recovery was far from completed before excess demand overtook us in the 1966–69 period'.[16]

Monetarism is difficult to apply. Different money concepts follow a different pattern. Velocity turns out to be capricious. But here again political factors influence policies. For example, President Reagan, the paladin of orthodox monetarist policy, promises a balance-of-payments equilibrium but cannot get rid of the highest deficit in the United States' history. Through a large budget deficit, in fact, he has pursued an expansionist fiscal policy. In the United States as in other countries, high real interest rates reflect the preemption of savings by governments.

In the United Kingdom monetary growth has been brought under control but unemployment and real interest rates remain high and profitability low. However, macroeconomic policies 'cannot on their own make a major contribution to reduction in unemployment over the medium term'.[17] Supply-side measures, especially those that promote more flexible labour markets, are needed.

But because monetary policy cannot provide short-term directives it is not to be put aside. 'Month-by-month, monetarism may have become a fickle guide. For the long haul, its rules look surprisingly useful'.[18]

In the OECD countries as a whole, monetary policy 'over the past few years has broadly speaking followed the prescriptions of the strategy: in general initially tight, it became less so as inflation came down'[19]: from a peak of 13 per cent in early 1980 to some 4.5 per cent at the end of 1985, the lowest rate for sixteen years. But again, when elections are approaching politicians plead for an easier monetary policy.

There are important areas of theory 'where little or no effect on policy'[20] is to be found (distribution) and there are economic policies with no origins in economic theory (aid to less developed countries), for which economic theory is even lacking (innovation) and which 'defy the rules of economics' (agricultural policy).[21]

Even in the few cases in which a policy seems to be based on economic theory, political pressures are needed to pursue that policy. Indeed, 'Theory will seldom be influential where it runs counter to a political interest that is clearly realized and efficiently organized'.[22]

Keynes's frequently quoted statement about the influence of economists seems to be wishful thinking: 'The ideas of economists and political philosophers both when they are right and when they are wrong are more powerful than is commonly understood'.[23] Roosevelt's New Deal, often called a Keynesian experiment, had nothing to see with Keynes or his theory.

But can we blame politicians for not taking economics as a serious matter? Can we blame them for being perplexed at the many divergent policies economists are advocating? Tinbergen's naîve but courageous call to put an end to the confrontation between 'monetarist, supply-side and deregulation economists and Keynesians'[24] is understandable.

5. ECONOMISTS' DISAGREEMENTS

Since theory can 'usually be made to support diverse policy solutions'[25] divergent opinions among economists are not surprising. Economists do not even agree about economic evolution in the past. Some attribute the Great Depression to a mistaken monetary policy (M. Friedman), others to a series of accidental factors (P.A. Samuelson). This explains why economists always disagree: 'Whenever I ask England's six leading economists a question', said Winston Churchill, 'I get seven answers – two from Mr. Keynes'.[26]

Hence G. Stigler's depressing conclusion: 'the economist's influence upon the formulation of economic policy has usually been small'.[27] To the question: 'How much credence should be attached to policy recommendations developed from contemporary economic theory?' E.J. Meehan answers: 'None'.[28]

Economic theory is not a book of recipes for all possible difficulties. Each economic phenomenon is unique and differs from preceding events. Hence knowledge of history is useful, but it does not necessarily offer a solution for current problems.

We cannot even speak of a *theory* of economic policy. It is an 'illusion to believe that through economic theory an infallible and exact economic policy is possible. Each decision will analytically and empirically be accompanied by a greater or a smaller margin of uncertainty' says P. Hennipman and he goes on: 'Besides scientific insight, an efficient policy requires experience, common sense, personal judgment, sense of proportion and other virtues which adorn the good statesman'.[29]

It implies that this statesman has understood the jargon of the economist, a jargon which does not facilitate communication with the rest of the population. 'In our age no subject matter lends itself better to solemn pedantry.'[30]

Precisely because 'personal judgment' is unavoidable, ideological factors cannot be excluded. Depending on the importance they attach to economic and political freedom, economists are on principle for or against the free market.

Experience shows out that a centrally planned economy operates far less efficiently than a market economy. Many politicians and trade union leaders call for more planning although they should be aware of the meagre results of planning in Eastern Europe. This means that personal judgment deliberately ignores experience.

How many have the nerve to admit their errors, as the former British prime minister J. Callaghan did in 1978 when he acknowledged that the Keynesian remedy (just spend your way out of a recession) was obsolete, and as President Mitterand did in 1983 after a similar experience?

The degree of independence that the economist can show is of extreme importance. An economist working for an employers' association never recommends an increase in companies' charges. An economist employed by a trade union refrains from proposing a decrease in wages. The economist in the civil service knows the kind of advice his minister expects. It is useless to make other proposals.

Hence the minor significance of advisory bodies in western countries. Instead of unanimous opinion the minister concerned receives a hotchpotch of opinions from the various groups. The minister could just as well attain those opinions directly from the groups concerned.

Where one should expect economists to be acting as paladins of independence, as in Parliament, one only finds mouthpieces of the various pressure groups. (Re)election prevails! There is nothing new under the sun. In 1949 L. von Mises observed that parliaments are populated by the representatives of most of the pressure groups. Among them are 'few for whom the nation counts more than their pressure group'.[31]

Universities should be the last bastions of independent thinking. But there too the candidates for appointments in semi-official and advisory bodies are numerous. Those appointments, however, are likewise reserved for the docile defenders of one or other special interest.

6. CONCLUSION

Economic theory has only a minor influence on economic policy. This is mainly the result of divergent (political) opinions among economists. Progression in tax rates, for example, has no foundation in economic theory but where are the economists' protests? Disagreement is unavoidable owing to ideological factors.

> Even identical choices of all relevant assumptions of fact would not secure agreement on policy recommendations if the advisers held different preferences in the pursuit of objectives.[32]

NOTES

1 A. Smith, *An inquiry into the nature and the causes of the wealth of nations* (London: s.n., 1776).

2 V. Pareto, *Cours d'économie politique,* pt. 2 (Lausanne: Rouge, 1897).
3 See J. de V. Graaff, *Theoretical welfare economics* (Cambridge: Cambridge University Press, 1957), pp. 142–52 for a survey of the 17 conditions that have to be fulfilled for the proposition to hold.
4 A. Downs, *An economic theory of democracy* (New York: Harper and Brothers, 1957).
5 F.A. Lutz, *Politische Überzeugungen und nationalökonomische Theorie* (Tübingen: J.C.B. Mohr, 1971), p. 50.
6 M.A.G. van Meerhaeghe, *Handboek van de economie,* 10th ed. (Antwerpen, Leiden: Stenfert Kroese, 1984), p. 339.
7 L.C. Thurow, op. cit., p. 49.
8 J.M. Keynes, op. cit.
9 P.A. Samuelson, Lord Keynes and the 'General Theory', *Econometrica,* July 1946, p. 190.
10 H.G. Johnson, Cambridge in the 1950s, *Encounter,* Jan. 1974, p. 39.
11 Cf. L.R. Klein, *The economics of supply and demand* (Baltimore: Johns Hopkins University Press, 1983).
12 M. Friedman, *The optimum quantity of money* (London: Macmillan, 1969), p. 47.
13 Bank for International Settlements, *46th Annual Report* (Basle, 1976), p. 134.
14 M. Friedman and A.J. Schwartz, *Monetary trends in the United States and the United Kingdom. Their relationship to income, prices and interest rates, 1867–1975* (Chicago: University of Chicago Press, 1982).
15 Bank of England Panel of Academic Consultants, *Monetary trends in the United Kingdom,* Panel Paper no. 22 (Bank of England, London Oct. 1983).
16 W.W. Heller, What's right with economics, *The American Economic Review,* March 1975, p. 14.
17 Organisation for Economic Cooperation and Development, *United Kingdom,* Economic Surveys 1984/85 (Paris, Jan. 1985), p. 51.
18 The year monetarism dies? *The Economist,* 4 Jan. 1986, p. 12.
19 Organisation for Economic Cooperation and Development, *OECD Economic Outlook,* Dec. 1985, p. viii.
20 C. Wilcox, From economic theory to public policy, *The American Economic Review,* May 1960, p. 29.
21 Ibid., p. 30.
22 Ibid., p. 35.
23 J.M. Keynes, op. cit., p. 383.
24 J. Tinbergen, De noodzaak van een synthese, *Economisch-Statistische Berichten,* Dec. 1982, p. 1284.
25 G. Stigler, op. cit., p. 131.
26 Quoted in B. Higgins, *What do economists know?* (Carlton: Melbourne University Press, 1951), p. 30.
27 G. Stigler, op. cit., p. 130.
28 E.J. Meehan, *Economics and policy making. The tragic illusion* (Westport Conn.: Greenwood Press, 1982), p. 129.
29 P. Hennipman, Doeleinden en criteria der economische politiek, in *Theorie van de economische politiek,* ed. J. Andriessen en M.A.G. van Meerhaeghe, op. cit. p. 77.
30 L. Rebatet, *Les décombres* (Evreux: Faivert, 1976), p. 234.
31 L. von Mises, op. cit., p. 866.
32 F. Machlup, *Methodology of economics and other social sciences* (New York: Academic Press, 1978), p. 383.

11. THE LIMITED PRACTICABILITY OF THE THEORY

In this chapter, we will discuss some limiting factors of economic theory.

1. ISOLATION FROM OTHER SCIENCES

From the preceding chapters we see that economics develops in marked isolation from the other sciences. In economics, there is little reference to results of recent research in, for instance, sociology, psychology, history and politicology. 'The contemporary economist is less of a jurist, less of a historian, less of a sociologist, less of a philosopher and less of an honest man than his predecessors. For him, economics is sufficient'.[1]

However, economic phenomena cannot be understood without a knowledge of the political and social circumstances under which they take place. The economy is not invariably the decisive factor: 'Never the sole and primary cause, economics is sometimes decisive: however, nothing guarantees that it will remain decisive even in identical situations'.[2]

W. Sombart even argued that 'any economic theory is ultimately sociology'.[3] J.M. Keynes, like many economists before him,[4] has stressed that the 'Master Economist must, to a certain degree, be a mathematician, a historian, a politician and a philosopher'.[5] A. Gray[6] believes that when he is merely an economist, 'he is damned'. G.L.S. Shackle chimes in with the assertion that to be a complete economist:

> a man needs only to be a mathematician, a philosopher, a psychologist, an anthropologist, historian, a geographer, and a student of politics; a master of prose exposition; and a man of the world with experience of practical business and finance, and understanding of the problems of administration, and a good knowledge of four or five foreign languages. All this in addition, of course, to familiarity with the economic literature itself.[7]

He adds that 'the good economist must be like a bottle of wine . . . he must mature'. If a 'complete economist' does not exist, every economist must nevertheless attempt to acquire a minimum knowledge of the related sciences.[8] Indeed:

> if the economist is not willing to study (certain political and social conditions), alone or together with the representatives of the other disciplines, he must renounce explaining economic phenomena, and give up advising in matters of political economy, except within very narrow limits.[9]

and K. Boulding goes even further: 'I have been gradually coming under the conviction, disturbing for a professional theorist, that there is no such thing as economics – there is only social science applied to economic problems'.[10] In fact, E. Malinvaud complains about 'the lack of proper theories for dealing with the interactions between economic and social developments'.[11]

For instance, expatiating on the role of trade unions is pointless without involving political and social considerations; the same applies to discoursing upon consumers' decisions without bringing in psychology.

As 'understanding of history ... one of the main requirements of the 'complete economist'[12] implies a critical attitude towards historical publications. One of the most persistent myths is that the industrial revolution and the rise of capitalism were disastrous for the working class. It is relatively easy to search the reports of the Royal Commissions and Committees of inquiry for details about the poor living conditions of the English labourers in the 18th century and the beginning of the 19th century. The 'historians' forget to add that compared with the pre-industrial period the standard of living did not decrease but even considerably increased from 1820 onwards.[13] The so-called drawbacks of capitalism were caused by monopolistic situations 'in fact due to remnants or revivals of precapitalistic features'.[14]

Furthermore, capitalism is not responsible for overpopulation. The resulting migration towards the cities caused housing problems ... but these also occurred in countries where there had been no industrial revolution.

Nobody claims that workmen led ideal lives during the industrial revolution, but the standard of living was not lower than before. The industrial revolution paved the way for an unprecedented improvement in living conditions. The greater concern about the workmen of that time did not mean that this standard had fallen or that before the industrial revolution the workmen had led an idyllic life.

The socialist interpretation of history is based – according to F. Hayek – on so-called 'facts which everybody knows' but 'have long been proved not to have been facts at all'.[15] He has in mind, for example, the so-called increase in monopolies and the so-called drawbacks of competition. (Crop surpluses have been mostly destroyed by government bodies.)

H. Johnson also deplores the political propaganda ladled out to the student, and more particularly the falsification of facts in many courses. Hence it is that a lecturer in international economics has to point out, concerning international relations that 'most of the beliefs that motivate national policies are irrational, most of the alleged facts are not facts, and most of the alleged lessons of experience are the results of ignorance or falsification of the actual facts of experience'.[16]

From the preceding discussion, it does not follow that economic theory did not progress as far as other social sciences. Sociology even deteriorates and sociological 'theory' seems to be limited to the setting up and commenting upon surveys. Moreover, sociology and especially political science often rely on economics. Consequently, it would be unwise to entertain too many illusions regarding closer cooperation with other sciences, the latter being in the grip of an even greater crisis situation than economics.

2. UNREALISTIC HYPOTHESES

Far too often, the theories we have studied proceed from unrealistic hypotheses. These include perfect competition, divisibility and substitutability of production factors, homogeneous goods, mobility of production factors and profit maximization. Equally reprehensible is the simplistic device of explaining economic phenomena by only one production factor (e.g. the Harrod-Domar theory). Even an analysis based on three production factors is scarcely an acceptable simplification. There are countless subdivisions of both skilled and unskilled labour. Capital goods, too, take various forms. Factor endowments vary from country to country and are unevenly spread. 'Economic models unrelated to reality are constructed, criticized, amended, on occasion commended and then alas, completely forgotten' complains J. Galbraith.[17] This is echoed by R.M. Cyert and C.L. Hedrick: 'The real world still escapes our models'.[18]

Nor can the marginalism that goes along with perfect competition account for the prices of goods, services and production factors. The concepts involved, such as marginal revenue, marginal product and marginal costs, cannot be calculated and for the most part they are actually unknown. Again and again the marginalists disregard the point that it is not the facts that must be made to fit the theory but *vice versa.* One of the functions of theory is to illustrate the real state of affairs: its purpose is not, as many think,[19] to study a world of abstractions.

a. Testing and falsifying

It is not enough to accept that hypotheses conform with reality – they need to be tested as well.[20] One can generally find observations to support a theory. If observations are consistent with the theory – and the hypotheses underlying a theory must be stated in such a way that they can be collated with the facts – this is still no proof that the theory is right. One can only prove that it is *not* right and therefore one must examine if the hypotheses have been falsified. According to K.R. Popper, theories that are not falsifiable belong to metaphysics, and not to an empirical science.[21]Thus, the assertion that a particular constitution cannot be maintained in the long run is not falsifiable, because no time limit is specified.[22]

After rejecting certain hypotheses, one must formulate others and ascertain whether they, too, are falsifiable. The progress of science depends on the interaction between the formulation of hypotheses and their rejection. T. Kuhn[23] does not entirely agree with the view that theories (paradigms) are constantly being adapted to the lessons of experience: at a certain moment in time, he claims, one theory is replaced by another, giving a better explanation. We see only a difference in degree between the two standpoints; in many cases they coincide.[24]

b. Nonoperational concepts

In this connection, the large number of nonoperational concepts in economics is to be deplored. Why concepts such as 'demand' and 'supply' are used, is a mystery. In reality, they cannot be quantified.

In economic analysis other concepts, which to a certain extent are determinable, are assumed to be constant (e.g. the marginal propensity to save, to consume and to import and technological knowledge in input-output analysis), whereas in point of fact, they sometimes fluctuate considerably. F. Machlup concludes a survey of the relevant problems as follows: '... while there are important numerical constants in the natural sciences, there are none in the social sciences',[25] since human beings 'have the awkward ability of being able to learn and modify their behaviour'.[26] Before 'they can begin to formulate better theories of a kind that are actually testable' economists 'will have to learn a great deal more about the behaviour of individuals in the economic aspects of their lives'.[27] In other words, we ought 'to value powers of observation more highly than powers of abstraction'.[28]

To assume that all phenomena involved in the argument are constant is dangerous: the *ceteris paribus* clause is a 'very tricky assumption'[29] and a 'slippery tool'.[30]

3. MATHEMATIZATION OF ECONOMICS

Economists often select the hypotheses on which to base their theories and models according to whether they can be represented by a preferably highly complex mathematical formula or graph. They operate from purely deductive principles (thinking they can proceed as would a mathematician or a physician).

Now mathematics can be a useful tool in stating economic problems, but today it is becoming an end in itself for some people – so much so that the 'nonmathematical practitioner is laboring under a dark suspicion (despite the history of economic thought) that nothing he does will be worthwhile'.[31] Much more than in 1932, when J. Robinson made the point, 'the subject matter of economics is neither more nor less than its own technique'[32] and we agree with L. Robbins when he says that:

> For all the proliferation of diagrams in recent literature, I doubt whether analytically, we have advanced very far beyond Marshall's few lines of algebra; and I suspect that, in practical judgment and sense of proportion, we are often some way behind'.[33]

A. Marshall himself formulated (not without humour) the following rules for the use of mathematics:

1. Use mathematics as a shorthand language, rather than as an engine of inquiry.
2. Keep to them till you have done.

3. Translate into English.
4. Then illustrate by examples that are important in real life.
5. Burn the mathematics.
6. If you can't succeed in 4, burn 3. This last I did often.[34]

In the same year as Robbins, F.D. Graham complained:

> All the inconvenient freight of fact has been discarded by the more recondite practitioners until the 'science' has come to move in a realm of pure abstraction useful for purposes of cerebration but of steadily declining practical importance'.[35]

Mathematical stylishness is preferred to convenience of calculation. Not the slightest thought is given to communicating with other economists, let alone with the intelligent layman.[36]

From the foregoing it follows that:

> the economists, and especially the econometrists, do not hesitate to launch new models on the scientific market without ascertaining empirically whether the new models are to be preferred to the old ones. In this way, the number of models increases rapidly, they become an encumbrance and contradict each other and they breed distrust and scepticism.[37]

'Economics has become a monstrous battlefield covered with ruins of models' – says E. Böhler – 'on each of which sits one economist in sublime solitude'.[38] Hence the following complaints: 'The whole economics profession ... is an example of that monumental misallocation of intellectual resources which is one of the most striking phenomena of our time'.[39] 'What is needed is a reallocation of economic brainpower towards the analysis and interpretation of the real world'.[40]

E.J. Mishan has given us a witty but accurate description of this kind of sport, and we cannot resist the temptation to reproduce it in full – with the permission of the author.

> To glance through the journals of the last ten or twenty years is to lose oneself in a carnival of possibility theorems. With so few empirical checks to speculative fervour the opportunities for economic science-fiction are practically boundless. One has only to outline the familiar routine of

> theory and counter-theory in economics to recognise, rather ruefully, the nature of the intellectual rake's progress involved. Thus, a well-known theory has it that, if we assume propositions *A, B* and *C,* it can be shown that *P then Q,* and *if R then S.* Some seminal mind now challenges this theory; to wit, if instead of *B* we assume *B**, and instead of *C* we assume *C**, we have the paradoxical result that *if P then S,* and *if R then Q*. It will not be long before it is pointed out that in the long run *B** tends to *B* and that *C** tends to *C,* at least if we make the reasonable assumption of *E.* A further contribution will reveal that if we introduce a new relationship, *G,* it no longer follows that *if P then Q,* and it will be concluded therefore that the original model has made the tacit assumption of non-*G.* This new contribution will therefore be regarded as a more general theory on the grounds that non-*G* is but the limiting case of *G*.
>
> In the same spirit another paper will introduce a further relationship *H* and conclude that all non-*H* models are special cases only. A controversy then begins about whether the proposition *H* is consistent with the *A* postulate: certainly it is not if we admit a fairly common assumption *F.* A new article now points out that the *A* postulate has been misunderstood; it has been misinterpreted as *A'*. In reply to this discovery, it will be insisted that *A'* is the proper interpretation. Generality of approach is promoted in a taxonomic paper that deduces the implications of *A*, of *A'*, and of both *A* and *A'* together. Someone writing for *Econometrica* will then juxtapose all the possibilities in matrix notation: depending on the conditions assumed the key variables can move in any direction. Somewhere else a literary digest of the controversy will be given and a new approach indicated. And so, notwithstanding occasional perorations of the what-we-need-is-some-systematic-empirical-investigation sort, the game goes on without respite. Economics has become the thing that economists write about, and as such it has become the science of infinite conjecture.[41]

Nothwithstanding 'the breakdown in . . . the economics profession's confidence in econometric results'[42] our students learn 'technique to the exclusion of the subject matter itself'[43] and when our graduates 'first assume practical responsibilities they have something to unlearn'.[44]

No more than the Nobel Prize in literature (from Sully-Preudhomme in 1901 to Golding in 1983) is the Nobel Prize in economics a guarantee for excellence. It reflects strongly the 'increased role of formalization and the increased use of mathematics'[45] in economic science. For one Kuznets, how many Debreus and other experts in models without any relation to relevant problems! In the list of the awards given since 1969 we search in vain for names such as Fritz Machlup (who died in 1982) and G. Haberler (born 1900).

4. CONCLUSION

We need not be surprised that there are complaints about the inapplicability of the theory: '. . . a major portion of our current articles are not useful for decisions – nor are they likely to form a base upon which future knowledge to improve decisions can be built'.[46] This grievance concerning monetary problems is valid for the entire field of economics. Some authors even wonder whether they have done a useful job.[47] If people were to ask themselves this question in advance, perhaps there would be less useless literature published. Of course, one can maintain with M. Friedman that the (empirical) unrealism of the theory 'itself', or of its 'assumptions', is quite irrelevant to its validity and worth,[48] but then – we repeat – we must recognise that what we are engaged in is art for art's sake.

NOTES

1 D. Villey, Examen de conscience de l'économie politique, *Revue d'Économie Politique,* Nov.–Dec. 1951, p. 851.

2 For instance, J.K. Ingram in 1878, The present position and prospects of political economy, in *Essays in economic method. Selected papers read to section F of the British Association for the Advancement of Sciences, 1869–1930,* ed. R.L. Smyth (London: G. Duckworth, 1962).

3 W. Sombart, *Nationalökonomie und Soziologie* (Jena: Gustav Fischer, 1930), p. 12.

4 J.P. Haesaert, *Sociologie générale* (Brussels – Paris: Erasme, 1956), p. 359.

5 Quoted in A. Gray, Economics: yesterday and tomorrow, *The Economic Journal,* Dec. 1949, p. 517.

6 Ibid., p. 517.

7 G.L.S. Shackle, *Uncertainty and other reflections* (Cambridge: Cambridge University Press, 1955), p. 24.

8 According to E.H. Phelps Brown, The underdevelopment of economics, *The Economic Journal,* March 1972, p. 8: 'the study of history forms an essential part of the training of the economist'.

9 C.P. Kindleberger in an introduction to M. Moret, *L'échange international* (Paris: Marcel Rivière, 1957), pp. 18–19.

10 K.E. Boulding, *A reconstruction of economics* (New York: John Wiley and Sons, 1950), p. vii.

11 E. Malinvaud, Positive economics in industrial countries. Paper read at the International Economic Association Conference on 'The relevance of economic theories to present-day society', Warsaw, June 19–24, 1978.

12 Niehans, Economics: history, doctrine, science, art, *Kyklos,* 1981, Fasc. 2, p. 166.

13 T.S. Ashton, The treatment of capitalism by historians, in *Capitalism and the historians,* ed. F.A. Hayek (Chicago: Univ. of Chicago Press, 1954). See also the articles by E.H. Phelps Brown and S.V. Hopkins in *Economica* (1955, 1956, 1957 and 1959) and a contribution on the same subject from D. Loschky, Seven centuries of real income per wage earner reconsidered, *Economica,* Nov. 1980.

14 F.A. Hayek, History and politics, in *Capitalism and the historians,* op. cit., p. 28.

15 *Ibid.,* p. 7.

16 H.G. Johnson, The role of international economics teaching in the analysis of international relations, in *International relations in a changing world* (Lyden: Sijthoff, 1977), p. 102.

17 J.K. Galbraith, *A contemporary guide to economics, peace and laughter,* ed. A.D. Williams (London: André Deutsch, 1971), p. 40.

18 R.M. Cyert and C.L. Hedrick, art. cit., p. 407.

19 See, e.g. J.G. Knol, *Facetten van de moderne prijstheorie* (Haarlem: De Erven F. Bohn N.V., 1965), pp. 12, 49.

20 H. Albert, Modell-Platonismus. Der neoklassische Stil des ökonomischen Denkens in kritischer Beleuchtung, in *Sozialwissenschaft und Gesellschaftsgestaltung. Festschrift für Gerhard Weiser,* ed. F. Karrenberg and H. Albert (Berlin: Duncker & Humblot, 1963).

21 K.R. Popper, *Logik der Forschung,* 2nd ed. (Tübingen: J.C.B. Mohr, 1966). English translation: *The logic of scientific discovery* (New York: Basic Books, 1959).

22 Example from A.D. de Groot, *Methodologie. Grondslagen van onderzoek en denken in de gedragswetenschappen,* 7th ed. ('s-Gravenhage: Mouton, 1972), pp. 99–100.

23 T. Kuhn, *The structure of scientific revolutions* (Chicago: University of Chicago Press, 1962).

24 Methodology can claim to attract a great deal of interest. See, e.g., *Criticism and the growth of knowledge,* ed. I. Lakatos and M. Musgrave (Cambridge: Cambridge Univ. Press, 1978) in which I. Lakatos interprets the history of science as a continuous competition between alternative research programmes (and not as a succession of conjectures and refutations or as paradigm-switches). See in this connection: *Method and appraisal in economics,* ed. S.J. Latsis (Cambridge: Cambridge Univ. Press, 1976), H. Katouzian, *Ideology and method in economics* (London: Macmillan, 1980), B.J. Caldwell, *Beyond positivism.* Economic methodology in the twentieth century (London: Allen & Unwin, 1982).

25 F. Machlup, Are the social sciences really inferior? *The Southern Economic Journal,* Jan. 1961, p. 179.

26 G.D.N. Worswick, Is progress in economic science possible?, *The Economic Journal,* March 1972, p. 83.

27 P. Deane, *The evolution of economic ideas* (Cambridge: Cambridge Univ. Press, 1978), p. 226.

28 E.H. Phelps Brown, The underdevelopment of economics, art. cit., p. 9.

29 S. Schoeffler, op. cit., p. 81.

30 A.F. Burns, *The frontiers of economic knowledge* (Princeton: Princeton University Press, 1954), p. 8.

31 M. Bronfenbrenner, A 'middlebrow' introduction to economic methodology, in *The structure of economic science,* ed. S.R. Krupp (Englewood Cliffs, N.J.: Prentice Hall, 1969), p. 9. See also R.L. Hall, Reflections on the practical application of economics, *The Economic Journal,* Dec. 1959, p. 651.

32 J. Robinson, *Economics is a serious object* (Cambridge: W. Heffer, 1932), p. 4.

33 L. Robbins, The economist in the twentieth century, *Economica,* May 1949, p. 97.

34 *Memorials of Alfred Marshall,* ed. A.C. Pigou. Reprints of economic classics (New York: Kelly and Millman, 1956), p. 427.

35 F.D. Graham, *Social goals and economic institutions* (Princeton: Princeton University Press, 1949), p. xvii.

36 R. Harrod, How can economists communicate? *The Observer,* July 24, 1969.

37 C. Gini, Au sujet de l'utilité et de la limitation de l'emploi du calcul des probabilitiés, *Economie Appliquée,* no. 1, 1957, p. 54.

38 E. Böhler, *Der Mythus in Wirtschaft und Wissenschaft* (Freiburg: Rombach, 1965), p. 20.

39 K.E. Boulding, The economics of knowledge and the knowledge of economics, *The American Economic Review,* May 1966, p. 12.

40 J.C. Odling-Smee, *The Economic Journal,* Sept. 1969, p. 588.

41 E.J. Mishan, Britain, the economist and the Six, *The Banker's Magazine,* Aug. 1962, p. 94.

42 L.C. Thurow, op. cit., p. 104.

43 G.D.N. Worswick, art. cit., p. 84.

44 E.H. Phelps Brown, art. cit., p. 2.

45 A. Lindbeck, The Prize in Economic Science in memory of Alfred Nobel, *Journal of Economic Literature,* March 1985, p. 54.

46 S.J. Maisel, The economic and finance literature and decision making, *The Journal of Finance,* May 1974, p. 313.

47 H.D. Evans, *A general equilibrium analysis of protection,* (Amsterdam: North Holland, 1972), p. x.

48 M. Friedman, *Essays in positive economics* (Chicago: University of Chicago Press, 1953).

12. THE SIGNIFICANCE OF ECONOMIC THEORY

Now that we have stressed the limited practicability of economic theory, it is appropriate to examine what significance it still has. First we will discuss the aspects of determinism and predictability.

I. DETERMINISM

Many authors do not accept economic phenomena as being determined. According to P. Hennipman, this is wrong; the determinism of phenomena really implies that 'they are subject to certain laws, known or unknown'.[1] Sensu stricto, facts are only explained from known laws. The fact that phenomena are determined or determinable is – still according to P. Hennipman – not to be confused with logical determinism of theoretical solutions or, in other words, with the logical determinism that occurs, if it is proved that the economic variable to be explained from variables of a theoretical model has a unique value. Mathematically speaking, the equality of the number of unknowns and the number of independent equations is a necessary but not a sufficient condition. Economic theory tries to find such determined solutions.

P. Hennipman explains why determinism founded on facts (empirical) and theoretical (logical) determinism do not necessarily coincide; in theoretical models:

a. Only the most important explanatory variables are considered (to prevent confusion). There remains an 'inexplicable residue one might call the marginal indeterminedness of phenomena'.[2]
b. The diversity of historical conditions that accompany phenomena is overlooked; the determined variables are different in every situation. ('Structural indeterminedness of facts' is the expression employed.) Yet each economic phenomenon is unique.[3]
c. No quantitative empirical results are obtained; it is not necessarily assumed that facts are available.

One must, however, take into consideration the fact that the 'policymaker' is only interested in empirical determinism, which is non-existent. In this connection we will deal with predictability.

2. PREDICTABILITY

In a sense, many economic statements are predictions: When in theory it is said that an increase in supply in a certain market, provided all other circumstances remain unchanged, leads to a drop in prices, one is predicting. When one speaks of predicting in economics, what one really means is assertions in connection with the course of, for instance, national income or the price level in the coming months or years.

The meagre balance of economics concerning these concrete predictions (in contrast with the theoretical, conditional predictions) is a fact. It is easy to compile extensive anthologies on erroneous predictions[4] of both national and international institutions, such as the European Economic Community, the European Coal and Steel Community, the Organisation for Economic Cooperation and Development. The phenomenon is not a new one. One need only point to experience obtained with the Harvard indicator. In Germany, it was predicted in 1933 that consumption of electricity in 1960 would amount to 32,000 million kWh. For the Federal Republic alone, consumption totalled 120,600 million kWh.[5]

From the empirical undeterminism of economic phenomena, it follows that making predictions is, if not impossible, at least very difficult; economic units do not necessarily maximize: Their reactions are unpredictable,[6] and furthermore, predictions sometimes influence the consumers' and producers' behaviour. It is too often assumed that many factors remain constant: If, for instance, the input-output table is used as an instrument of prediction, a proportional relation between inputs and outputs is assumed (technological knowledge remaining the same). This is scarcely a realistic hypothesis. That no influence is exerted by prices on the technological coefficients (as is implicitly assumed) is also improbable.

The specialized institutes – and there are hundreds of them in the world – whose predictions are based on extensive models do not achieve any better results. They 'are always one inflation too late in specifying the exact form of the price forecasting equations'.[7] Generally speaking, even in the best institutions the data obtained are very often changed arbitrarily, being based on 'feeling'. There are too many psychological and political variables (which influence the anticipations of the economic units) to insert them all in the models. D.B.J. Schouten correctly believes that:

> ... any forecast concerning the pattern of the business cycle has only a limited value. Even the best-equipped cyclical-research bureau is unable at the present time to construct a reliable business-cycle prognosis for any longer period than a year.[8]

I do not believe predicting to be part of economic science's task: It already has its hands full describing and explaining (unique) economic phenomena. Hence, to condemn economics because of its failure to predict – as S. Schoeffler does[9] – cannot be upheld.

This view does not imply that the economist should not make predictions: However, the economist must state explicitly the large number of (unrealistic) hypotheses on which the predictions – in most cases extrapolations – are based.

The fact that predicting is considered part of the task of economics sometimes influences the formulation of assumptions. Thus, Milton Friedman thinks that 'the only relevant test of *validity* of a hypothesis is comparison of its predictions with experience',[10] in other words:

> ... the relevant question to ask about 'assumptions' of a theory is not whether they are descriptively 'realistic', for they never are, but whether they are sufficiently good approximations for the purpose at hand. And this question can be answered only by seeing whether the theory works, which means whether it yields sufficiently accurate predictions.[11]

Friedman incorrectly believes that every abstraction assumes the use of false assumptions;[12] he does not, however, explain why the difference between assumptions and reality is of no importance.[13] If Friedman's point of view is accepted, practically any theory could be formulated (falsifying the assumptions being impossible; moreover, the theory must be consistent). Finally, the prediction itself is not explained. W. Leontief argues that 'The prevalence of such a point of view is, to a large extent, responsible for the state of splendid isolation in which our discipline nowadays finds itself'.[14]

3. THEORY OR METHOD?

Economic life is so complex and varied that the theory cannot take into account all the data available. It is obliged to simplify – to assume, for instance, that many factors remain constant (the *ceteris paribus* clause). The more we try to reduce it to a meaningful pattern, the less we succeed in truly reflecting the real world. Nevertheless, many economists are 'totally unconscious that their reasonings cannot, at one and the same time, be rigorous and yet capable of seizing all the essentials of reality'.[15] Hence, H.G. Johnson's view that 'if economic theory is to be applied to problems of economic policy this can most usefully be done within the context of a particular problem occurring in a particular environment'.[16] If we take simplification too far, he adds, theory can be more of a hindrance than a help. R. Triffin, too, points out that economic science, conceived otherwise:

> disencumbered, ... of all the ... limitations and taboos implied in the classical assumptions ... will recognize the richness and variety of all concrete cases, and tackle each problem with due respect for its individual aspects.[17]

However much we may regret it, the fact remains that economics is of little empirical consequence. In a sense, economics is, to quote yet again the somewhat overstated view of Lord Keynes, 'a method rather than a doctrine, an apparatus of the mind, a technique of thinking'.[18]

4. CONCLUSION

It may be objected that the occasionally sharp criticism we have levelled against various concepts and theories has been purely negative (since we have offered nothing as a substitute). However, this is no reason for continuing to uphold theories that are untenable. Furthermore, if we proceed from what has been said above we may doubt whether there *is* any substitute, whether a *general* economic theory is at all possible.

> It is in no way impossible that the difficulties encountered time and again by economic analysis are inherent in the subject matter of economics, that perfect solutions are out of reach, and that there is no method which can

> supply the certainty which is so often required from economics. But even if this is so, there is no cause for casting serious doubts on its significance and future.[19]

At any rate, the self-assurance evident in many publications and statements by economists often seems misplaced to us.

> The self-assurance accruing to any profession handling its subject mathematically has overtaken economists. With feelings of great confidence in this 'scientific' approach, they have developed a compensating distrust, indifference, if not disdain, towards the findings obtained by non-mathematical methods in other sciences.[20]

The layman is given the impression that economics is capable of solving all problems. Many economists simply will not admit that in many cases there just is no precise answer. What J. Tinbergen says with reference to the optimum savings' function:

> If is characteristic of the underdeveloped state of our science that virtually nothing empirical is known about this generalization and that, as a consequence, nothing sensible can be said about the optimum level of savings at present[21]

holds well, as our contribution will have shown, not only for this concept. We do not deny that economic science has advanced over the last twenty or thirty years, but the advice presented by F. Simiand in 1937 still applies: 'What economic science should be working on at the moment is realizing how very little it knows. This is perhaps the step forward that would do it most good'.[22]

Defeatism? No, realism:

> Even when it is not possible to give a complete explanation of the phenomena, to find all-embracing exact laws or to attain omniscience, thorough theoretical and empirical research is never pointless. A classification of possibilities, an orderly arrangement of the most important elements, the identification of important relations may, even when they do not solve all questions, increase perception sufficiently to be useful in practice. Knowing something is always better than knowing nothing.[23]

Besides, even 'in its present state (the science of economics yields) a considerable number of viewpoints which are of great scientific and practical value'.[24]

NOTES

1 P. Hennipman, art. cit., p. 255.
2 P. Hennipman, art. cit., p. 256.
3 Cf. Niehans, art. cit., p. 166.
4 M.A.G. van Meerhaeghe, La planification indicative, in *Les problèmes de la planification,* Colloque de janvier 1962 (Brussels: Université Libre de Bruxelles-Institut de Sociologie, 1963), pp. 48–51.
5 H. Wilhelm, Instrumentale Wirtschaftstheorie und rationale Wirtschaftspolitik, *Zeitschrift für die Gesamte Staatswissenschaft,* Heft 3, 1967, p. 547.
6 See in this connection J. Goudriaan, *Economie in zestien bladzijden of inleiding tot de analytische economie* (Amsterdam: de Bussy, 1952).
7 O. Eckstein, *Business Week,* June 29, 1974, p. 53.
8 D.B.J. Schouten, *Dynamische macro-economie,* Pt. 1, *Conjunctuurtheorie,* (Leiden: Stenfert Kroese, 1967), p. 168.
9 S. Schoeffler, op. cit., p. 41.
10 M. Friedman, *Essays in positive economics,* op. cit., pp. 8–9.
11 Ibid., p. 15.
12 J. Melitz, Friedman and Machlup on the significance of testing economic assumptions, *Journal of Political Economy,* Feb. 1965, pp. 40–41.
13 T.C. Koopmans, *Three essays on the state of economic science* (New York: McGraw-Hill, 1957), pp. 137–138.
14 W. Leontief, Theoretical assumptions and nonobserved facts, *The American Economic Review,* March 1971, p. 5.
15 G.L.S. Shackle, in a Book Review in *The Economic Journal,* Dec. 1967, p. 859.
16 H.G. Johnson, The taxonomic approach to economic policy, *The Economic Journal,* Dec. 1951, p. 828.
17 R. Triffin, *Monopolistic competition and general equilibrium theory* (Cambridge, Mass.: Harvard University Press, 1940), p. 189.
18 J.M. Keynes, in the introduction to the 'Cambridge Economic Handbooks'.
19 P. Hennipman, art. cit., p. 264.
20 W.I. Greenwald, Common irrelevancies in the contemporary theorizing by economists, *Kyklos,* fasc. 3, 1957, p. 305.
21 J. Tinbergen, Optimum savings and utility maximization over time, *Econometrica,* April 1960, p. 489.
22 Quoted by R. Miry, art. cit., p. 359. See also H. Guitton: 'It is necessary to develop economic science which is still in its infancy, far more than to rehabilitate economic policy', (Est-ce nécessaire de réhabiliter l'économie politique?, *Revue d'Économie Politique.* Jan.-Feb. 1975, p. 141).
23 P. Hennipman, art. cit., p. 262.
24 Ibid., p. 264. In this connection, attention should be drawn to the national accounts, which give a clear picture of the main real and financial flows between the various economic units.

Index of authors

Index of subjects

MIX
Papier aus verantwortungsvollen Quellen
Paper from responsible sources
FSC® C105338

If you have any concerns about our products,
you can contact us on
ProductSafety@springernature.com

In case Publisher is established outside the EU,
the EU authorized representative is:
Springer Nature Customer Service Center GmbH
Europaplatz 3, 69115 Heidelberg, Germany

Printed by Libri Plureos GmbH
in Hamburg, Germany